Bygone
Seaton Carew

An Illustrated History

BYGONE

Seaton Carew

AN ILLUSTRATED HISTORY

MAUREEN ANDERSON

Wharncliffe Books

First Published in Great Britain in 2004 by
Wharncliffe Local History
an imprint of
Pen and Sword Books Ltd.
47 Church Street
Barnsley
South Yorkshire
S70 2AS

Copyright © Maureen Anderson, 2004

ISBN: 1-903425-93-X

Typeset in 11/13pt Plantin by Mac Style Ltd, Scarborough.
Printed and bound in England by
CPI UK.

Pen and Sword Books Ltd incorporates the Imprints of
Pen & Sword Aviation, Pen & Sword Maritime,
Pen & Sword Military, Wharncliffe Local History,
Pen & Sword Select, Pen and Sword Military Classica
and Leo Cooper.

For a complete list of Pen & Sword titles please contact
PEN & SWORD BOOKS LIMITED
47 Church Street
Barnsley
South Yorkshire
S70 2BR
England
E-mail: enquiries@pen-and-sword.co.uk
Website: www.pen-and-sword.co.uk

Contents

Cover Acknowledgements:
Front (Upper Image): Pattison's Pictures
Front (Lower Image): *Seaton Carew from the Common*, Ellen Pearson, c1850
Hartlepool Arts & Museum Collection

Introduction

This publication takes the reader from a time before the existence of settled communities up to the twentieth century. Pattison's photos and images and maps and sketches from other sources give a visual history of Seaton Carew from its beginnings. Through the years Seaton Carew seems to have risen and fallen again eventually establishing itself as a tiny hamlet then growing to a village and finally becoming part of a thriving town.

The eighteenth and nineteenth centuries were a time when every natural source was utilised for the survival of the people. Sea-coal, wood and cargo from shipwrecks, shellfish and fish, as well as what could be grown, was harvested. In those years farming, fishing and catering for visitors were the main occupations of the villagers. With the port of Hartlepool and, later West Hartlepool developing, Seaton Carew had its share of wealthy landowners and benefactors. Solicitors, ship owners, merchants and doctors made their homes in the village far enough away from the hustle and bustle of Hartlepool whilst still being close to their places of work.

At the time most of these photographs were taken the village was the best known in all of South Durham. In the summer months, a resort for both the very young and the very old, the absence of dangerous cliffs and the extensive beach of firm sand, commended it to parents as a place to take their little ones, while the grandparents enjoyed it as a place of charm and peace. The sea rolled away into the distance; vessels sailed to and from the adjacent ports; fleets of tiny fishing craft spread their sails making for the fishing grounds and now and again a little wisp of smoke could be seen from an outward bound steamer fast disappearing over the horizon on its way to some distant foreign port. To the north the town of Hartlepool looked as though one could reach out and touch it. To the south, the magnificent grandeur of the Cleveland (Land of Cliffs) Hills dotted here and there with tiny white houses. Redcar, Saltburn and Marske were plainly discernable in the distance. Westward were the fertile uplands, the monotony of the fields relieved by clumps of trees and the fluttering arms of the occasional windmill. Boys played cricket on the Green, football and golf on the Snook.

The winter months told a different story, when lives were snuffed out merely by a change in the direction of the wind; when the little white-capped waves became thundering breakers pushing everything in their path before them; when the cries of the lost souls could be heard as they fell from their wooden ships into the churning brine beneath them and were lost far from their homes and loved ones.

Amongst early photographers that captured images in the North East was Francis Frith who had set up a studio in 1860 and travelled all over Britain building a huge collection of images. These were then bought by millions of Victorians as the perfect souvenir of a place they had visited. Frith first visited Seaton Carew, Hartlepool and the surrounding area in 1886. His two sons, Eustace and Cyril, who followed in his footsteps, came to the area towards the end of the nineteenth century. In 1902, three years after Frith's death, the picture postcard appeared and the Frith archive became an even more thriving multi-million pound business. The collection was added to from around 1955–65 when other photographers from the company travelled around Britain to update the archives. There are fifteen Frith images of Seaton Carew dating from 1886 to 1965. Nearly all of Frith's images, although a wonderful record of past times, are of buildings, streets and beaches with very few of people. A famous local collection was the work of Frank Meadow Sutcliffe who set up a gallery in 1875. Most of his images are of everyday life and people in Whitby. Pattison's collection is on a smaller scale than those of Frith and Sutcliffe but the subject content is of an equal quality. Perhaps it was Francis Frith that inspired Pattison to take up the hobby of photography. The two men were certainly in the village at the same time and someone like Frith arriving in the tiny community with all his photography paraphernalia would not have gone unnoticed. Whatever the reasons for James Pattison taking up the hobby I am sure the reader will agree that the images in this publication are a truly remarkable example of photography when it was still in its infancy.

Newspaper articles and old records are sometimes incomplete or conflicting but every effort has been made to ensure that the information given in this publication is accurate.

My sincere thanks to all of the following: Deborah Anderson and the staff of the Archaeology Department and Bowes Museum for allowing me to research and use these wonderful images from Pattison's Pictures; Gary Green, of Tees Archaeology, and Charlotte Taylor, of Hartlepool Arts and Museums, without whose help much of the history would have been incomplete; Brian Elliott, Commissioning Editor, and the staff at Wharncliffe for putting together the finished article; John 'Harry' Harrison for his assistance at the final stages and to my husband, Jim, for his encouragement and patience.

Chapter One

Pattison's Pictures

The Reverend John Lawson, who was lucky enough to be one of the 'landed gentry,' became vicar of Holy Trinity Church in Seaton Carew in 1835 and remained so until his death at the age of eighty-two. There are records of curates being involved with the church from 1875, presumably because, by then, the Reverend was in his twilight years and needed assistance in the day to day running of his parish. James Whitehead Pattison, who had been ordained in 1882, was one such curate assigned to the parish in 1885, where he remained until October 1890. He then moved to Dinsdale, near Darlington, until 1897. Pattison became curate alongside J Wood and to the Reverend W Lonney at St James Church in Portrack Lane East in Stockton. In 1906 he was made vicar of St John's Chapel in Weardale and was there until his retirement in 1925. Pattison was born in Leeds in 1853 and died at Weardale in 1936. Married to Harriet Elizabeth, his first daughter, Catherine, was baptised on 18 November 1885, his second daughter, Hilda, was baptised on 25 May 1888 both baptisms were performed by Reverend Lawson in Holy Trinity Church.

James Pattison, on the left of the image, playing chess with John Lawson in 1887. Pattison's Pictures

James Pattison leans on a gate reading a magazine while another clergyman gazes into the distance, 1888. Pattison's Pictures

Pattison took up the hobby of photography in 1887. A man that obviously had a great love of people, he took photographs of everyday life and by doing so, whether it was purely for enjoyment or with foresight, he has left a wonderful record of the working classes and their surroundings from 1887 until the early twentieth century. Famous people are often immortalised on

Pattison's caption 'My first photo'. The family group portrays the same gentleman as in the previous image, 1887. Pattison's Pictures

Catherine and Hilda Pattison carrying their spades on the sands at Seaton in 1889.
Pattison's Pictures

canvas or film but Pattison has left a timeless legacy of ordinary people, many of them poor and illiterate. Their images will survive forever because of the interest this remarkable man took in the people of his parish.

The collection includes Pattison's own photographs and glass plate negatives of Scotland and England, sketches and photographs given to him by others, cards sent to his daughter, Catherine, and copies of pictures

An appealing study of Catherine Pattison at three years of age. Catherine presented her father's collection to Bowes Museum in about 1973. Pattison's Pictures

from illustrated newspapers. There is also a love story, set between Hartlepool and Blackhall, entitled *Graciosa* written by John Lawson.

Pattison's later photos were of Weardale, mainly St John's Chapel, and include many natural poses of children. The collection is held by the Bowes Museum at Barnard Castle to whom it was presented by Catherine Pattison in about 1973. This compilation of images of Seaton Carew from Pattison and other sources show, not just the picture postcard view of a summer resort, but

Pattison's house with the Staincliffe to the left of the image in 1889. The grass at the front of the houses was used for grazing cattle and sheep. Looking very different now, the house still stands on the corner of Lawson Road and Queen Street. The iron railings were removed for the war effort but the holes where they were once imbedded can still be seen. Pattison's Pictures

The Italian Hurdy Gurdy man outside Pattison's house in 1889. Everyone looked forward to the arrival of these travelling hawkers. Besides sharpening knives, they carried penny books and unusual wares. A bird in a cage is being taken from the cart to show the little crowd of onlookers. Pattison's Pictures

The drawing room of Pattison's house in 1889. The heavy fabrics, wallpaper and clutter were typical décor of the Victorian era. Pattison's Pictures

give a rare insight into the development of the village. Many of Pattison's photos had pencil written captions on them. Where they could be deciphered they have been added to the captions included in this publication.

'See, I can reach the knocker, bet you can't!' Pattison's Pictures

'*Aw, come on don't sulk, we were only joking with you*'. Pattison's Pictures

'*I wish you'd stop that racket. I can't concentrate on writing on my slate*'. Pattison's Pictures

'*Hurry up with your homework and come play with me*'. Pattison's Pictures

Chapter Two

In The Beginning

Ten thousand years ago the landscape of Cleveland was still emerging from the ice. What is now the North Sea was once low-lying fenland. The rising sea is now covering these landscapes but at certain low tides a large area of submerged forest, between Hartlepool and Seaton, and also at Redcar, is still visible. Trees, branches, twigs and even hazel nuts embedded in the clay, can be clearly seen when the sand is swept away. Peat covered this area roughly 7,000 years ago, 1,000 years later the sea inundated the land. Perhaps 1,000 years later still, the sea fell back again and more peat began to form. On each occasion shallow, freshwater pools would have been left and trees, such as alder, oak, hazel and elm, began to take root in these bogs

Charles Taylor 'Otto' Trechmann was a geologist who did a study and photographed parts of the submerged forest in 1936 and 1947. His findings included Mesolithic flints, bones and antlers of red deer. The Mesolithic people, from around 8,000 to 3,000 BC, did not have permanent settlements but followed the game over wide areas. Trechmann's and subsequent finds show that these people hunted in this area when it was still mainly forest. In about 3,000 BC, the Neolithic people were living a more settled existence. The trees were now in decline and there was an increase in grassland plants. Charcoal was found indicating that early farmers used fire to manage the land. As farming developed from about 2,000 BC, more clearing took place reducing the woodland by about two thirds of its natural extent. Round barrows were used as territorial markers and for the burial of people of high status and then there was the gradual introduction of bronze. By the first century AD, the time of the Roman Conquest, the area had a substantial scattering of Iron Age farmsteads and hamlets. Cattle and pig bones have been found showing that the early settlers kept domestic animals. One bone was found with the indentations of teeth marks believed to be from Hartlepool's earliest known dog. Early pottery fragments and a lid with a wooden handle were also discovered. In 1971 the skeleton of a Neolithic man was found on the beach. It is believed by archaeologists to have been a deliberate burial. The body had been placed on the surface of the peat in a crouched position on his right side. Near his right elbow a small group of flint flakes had been placed and there was evidence that the body had been covered with twigs or branches of birch. The man had suffered a blow to the skull, probably with a blunt axe. He had broken ribs but these had healed before death. The teeth were worn but not decayed, no sweets or fizzy drinks in those days! There have been a number of finds of these deliberate burials in

A recumbent tree from the remains of the submerged forest that still exists beneath the sand between Hartlepool and Seaton. Photo by CT Trechmann, 1936. Hartlepool Arts and Museums Collection

Scandinavia believed to have some religious or ceremonial significance. The Seaton skeleton is one of only a small number to be found in the whole of Europe.

Cleveland County Archaeology carried out an excavation in 1990 and another when the sea defences were to be renewed from Carr House Sands to Seaton Carew in 1994. On the upper part of the beach near Newburn Bridge a line of wooden stakes was found, thought to be part of a fence or a hurdle. This structure, along with discoveries of worked flints, a cut piece of antler and some domestic rubbish suggested a settlement close by. Other finds were of Roman metal work, a wattle panel dated to the fourth millennium BC and wooden stakes set out in such a way that they were probably used for fishing. During the construction of the sea defences the contractors exposed a human skeleton within the dune sand of the old promenade. When excavated it was found that some of the skeleton had been disturbed by the contractor's machinery. The feet were missing, perhaps due to dune slumping at that end of the grave. Analysis of the bones showed this had been a man about 1.64m tall that died in middle to late life. The lower front teeth showed a distinct concave wearing which was probably caused by constantly having a clay pipe in his mouth. A piece of clay pipe was found adjacent to the left leg. The body was under the old promenade which was completed in 1905. All the evidence suggested the burial took place between the post-medieval period and the very early nineteenth century.

In about 1823 Edward Pease of Darlington observed some black earth to the north of Seaton where the tides had washed the sand away. He found a Roman spearhead and a brass coin of Domitian (81–96 AD). In

The skeleton of a Neolithic man found on Seaton beach in what was thought to be a deliberate, perhaps ritual, burial. The bones are now on display in Hartlepool Museum. The Author

September of 1885 it was reported that Mr RM Middleton found the remains of a Roman wall at Carr House. Henry Casebourne and Edward Pease had found Roman artefacts and coins. Robert Chilton, the keeper of the low lighthouse, and an agricultural labourer, Potter, also possessed Roman relics.

A report in the *South Durham Herald* in 1879 read:

Unfortunately the memorable record commonly called the Doomsday Book does not include the County of Durham and in consequence we have no reliable information as to the history of 'Seaton' at that remote period. The Bishop of Durham, Ethelwin, at the time of the Norman Conquest, opposed the royal authority and was helped by Malcolm III of Scotland in his rebellion. This monarch afterwards continued to harass the northern provinces, and in one of his predatory irruptions penetrated as far as Cleveland and from thence to the eastern parts of Durham spreading universal desolation. Not even the edifices sacred to religion were spared. They who fled into the churches for refuge were burned in their imagined sanctuary, and so great was the number of captives, that for many year, they were found in every Scottish village, nay in every Scottish hovel. In this expedition he laid waste the territory of Hertness, the country and forests around the present Hartlepool. John Speed, in his History of Great Britain, tells us that William I to arrest the progress of Malcolm's invasion: Wasted all the faire countrie betwixt Yorke and Durham, leaving all desolate for three-score miles space, which nine years after lay untilled; and with scarcely any inhabitants, when grew so great famine that these northerns were forced to eat the flesh of men.

So much for the locality of Seaton Carew in those days, whether the shrewd characteristics of its inhabitants are inherited from their forefathers who were exiled to the land o'cakes, whether their sturdy physique is owing to their progenitors having had to endure the hardships described above, and whether the chapel dedicated to Sir Thomas a'Beckett, of which we read at a later period, was then in existence for the people to fly to for fancied safety, are points upon which history is silent. All that can be said is that there is a great probability about such conjectures.

In April 1941 elephant bones were found buried on the beach and in 1948 the villagers were asked to 'plant' their used Xmas trees on the beach to help prevent erosion to the dunes. I wonder if they grew!

Chapter Three

Landowners

The earliest proof we have of landowners is that they were Saxons. It is recorded that Styr, son of Ulphus, gave lands to the see (diocese) of Durham in the time of Aldune, the first Bishop, who was born in about 963 AD. The records that follow are that, after the Norman Conquest, the lands then came into the hands of Robert de Brus who married the daughter of Fulk de Panell. She was heiress to property in Hart and Hartness. In about 1135 a knight named Robert de Carrowe was Lord of the Manor of Seaton. Peter Carrowe in 1180, it is recorded in the King's Charter to Bishop Pudsey:

To hold his Lordship of the Crown by the service of one knight's fee; which service he and his heirs are awarded from henceforth to render to the see of Durham, as the other Bishop's tenants between Tyne and Tees.

The Bishop of Durham gave lands in Seaton to Merton College in Oxford when it was founded in 1264. This comprised of five and a quarter stints on Seaton Snook. The Carrowe's and their heirs held much of the land until the fifteenth century. In the fourteenth century the family of Seton held land called 'Maisterionland' or Masterland. This land consisted of waste messuage (dwelling), six cottages and about 100 acres of land. Thomas Seton, who died in about 1359, had a daughter, Alice, who married Sir Thomas Carrowe and gave birth to John. He was to be the last male heir with the name of Carrowe when he died childless in 1387. The Lumley, Seton and Sayer families were the main descendants, either by marriage or blood through aunts and uncles, of the family of Carrowe. On John's death, Sybil, the wife of John Conyers, John Hayton and Thomas Lumley were his heirs. They were entitled to all his land in Seaton except

Sketch of Franklin's Corner and Carr House by Miss Parish, c1845. Pattison's Pictures

A view of the village from a lithograph, possibly by Ellen Pearson, c1850. Author's Collection

for Masterland. The estate was held in dower by Isabel Umfraville. On her death Masterland passed to Thomas Lumley and John Sayer. The Sayer's portion stayed in their hands until 1638 when two dwellings and 280 acres were passed to Robert Johnson. John Hayton and his wife passed their land to Ralph, Earl of Westmoreland, who in turn passed land to John Lumley. The two dwellings and the 280 acres that were held by Robert Johnson became united with another portion of the manor. A small estate consisting of one dwelling, six acres of land, a saltpit and two oxgangs (as much as an ox could plough in a year, between thirteen and twenty acres) was held by a kinsman of John Carrowe in 1345. The kinsman's grandson died about 1407 leaving a daughter, Alice, who married Robert Lambton. This family held the estate until at least 1612.

Seaton Carew from the common in 1850 from a lithograph by Ellen Pearson. Little is known about this Greatham artist but she is credited with a lithograph portrait of Ralph Ward Jackson. Hartlepool Arts and Museums Collection

Sketch of Carr House and Carr Cottages at the northern end of the village with Hartlepool in the distance by Margaret Lawson, John Lawson's daughter, c1850. Pattison's Pictures

Avice, the third co-heir of John Carrowe, was married twice. Her heir was her son by her first marriage, Thomas Langton. In about 1425 she left quarter of the manor of Seaton and other estates. Thomas was the Lord of Wynyard in Grindon, his estate followed the descent of Wynard until the division among the heirs in the sixteenth century. These co-heirs sold their portions to Robert Johnson of Oughton in about 1612. Johnson also bought the fourth quarter of the manor which had been assigned to Joan Carrowe in 1387. In 1620 the main parcels of land were owned in Seaton by Sir William Reed of Middlesex, Sir Henry Anderson of Elemore Hall and the Johnsons. In about 1731 Anthony Johnson and his wife, Catherine, conveyed four dwellings and about 240 acres of land in Seaton and Hartlepool with an eighth part of the manor of Seaton to John Simpson. In 1684 the freeholders within Seaton were: Robert Johnson, John Dodsworth, William Lee of Stockton, William Johnson of Claxton, George Williamson, William Corker, Thomas Hett, Anthony Johnson, Nicholas Johnson and the heirs of William Bellasis of Oughton. In 1638 a quarter of the manor was settled on Nicholas Johnson, son of Robert. This included Tofts Farm which stayed within the family for more than a hundred years. James Johnson added to the estate and in 1730 left it to his brothers. The estate was sold in 1750 to William Metcalf. It passed down through his family until 1828 when it was passed to trustees to sell. The second Lord John Eldon bought Red Barn in 1831 from Edward Robinson and Tofts Farm in 1832. In 1849 he purchased Golden Flatts Farm, Hunter House Farm, comprising 600 acres of land, and a salmon fishery on the River Tees and one on the sea. Some of the other landowners and tenants from the

Sketch by Margaret Lawson looking south to the northern end of the village showing Carr House and cottages, c1850. Pattison's Pictures

seventeenth to the nineteenth century were: John and Robert Wilson, Christopher and John Fulthorpe, Robert Gibson, Margrit and Christopher Maire, Joseph and Catherine Hall, Lancelot and James Carr, Thomas Rudd, George Hutton, Robert and Margery Preston, Thomas Cragg, William Estob, George Sutton, George Hutchinson, Joseph Lamb, Robert Allison, George Brown, George Hunter, William Robinson, George Hutton Wilkinson, John and Joseph Elstob, Robert Chilton, James and Edward Backhouse, Thomas Short, Christopher and William Wray, John and Jane Forster, William and Mary Metcalf, Robert Henry McDonald, Robert and Mary Lumley and the Pattison family. In the early twentieth century the principal landowners were William Thomlinson, Lord John, the Earl of Eldon and the Boddy family.

Dwellings and land would often be owned by more than one person and leased out. An example of this is Bath House at South End. The house and other cottages, stables and paddock were owned from 1838 to 1841 by William Chaytor, Rev John Wilkinson, George and Jane Wilkinson, Thomas Crawford and Ralph Ward Jackson. One of the descendants of Thomas Crawford sold the house in 1922 to William Thomlinson.

Chapter Four

The Early Village & Transport

The word Carew derives from the Carrowe family. Seaton probably comes from sea-town or on-sea. From 1146 there have been different spellings recorded including; Setone, Sethon, Seton Carrewe and Seton Kerrowe. William Longstaffe, the historian, was recorded as saying that the title could have come from a Saxon word for the village 'Ceattun':

> *The parish of Stranton originally comprised the townships of Brierton, Seaton Carew and Stranton; it was bounded on the north and north-west by the parish of Hart, on the south-west by Elwick Hall, on the south by Greatham and on the east by the German Ocean. In 1841 Seaton Carew was constituted a distinct chapelry.*

The boundary at the beginning of the nineteenth century between Seaton and Stranton was the White Dyke, a wall that was thought to date from Roman times. The southern boundary was a little stream at Teesmouth

A cart-track along the top of the cliffs was the route from Seaton to Hartlepool. In bad weather conditions the cliffs would take the full force of the sea and were badly eroded. They were eventually levelled off and a road was built on the reclaimed land. Author's Collection

Cottages and houses on Front Street in 1853. The image shows how the sea came almost to the back doors before the breakwaters were built. The Royal Café is on the far end of the row. The centre house was used as a post office and grocer's shop. Photograph by Edward Backhouse. Pattison's Pictures

Franklin's Corner in 1853 showing the wall in which the old cannon was embedded. Photo by Edward Backhouse.
Pattison's Pictures

The same view of Franklin's Corner in 1888 showing the changes to the roadway. Pattison's Pictures

A view to the south along Front Street showing the Seaton Hotel at the end of the row. On the left of the view White's Café had become the Oriental Café and later became the Dovecote Cafe. The building once housed a small cinema upstairs. It has also been a general dealers, tobacconist and gift shop, c1900 Author's Collection

A view to the south along Front Street showing the Seven Stars on the centre right of the image and the Seaton Hotel at the end. The building on the left was built in 1894 and the sign states 'White's Café,' c1894. Author's Collection

known as Wambling's Run. There was also a boundary post on the sea-shore. The custom of 'riding the boundaries' was still carried out in Seaton up to the early nineteenth century.

From at least 1740, and probably earlier, the 'road' north from Seaton was a cart track that went through the farmyards of Carr House and Cliff House avoiding the steep sides of the narrow dean by taking to the beach. A track then led through New Stranton, over Stranton Snook and on to Middleton. This narrow track remained until the 1880s. In about 1871 the project for a direct road between Hartlepool and Seaton was planned but it met huge opposition on the grounds that it was expensive and unnecessary. It was not until 1882, when Seaton lost its independence and became part of West Hartlepool, that a road was eventually built linking the two. The southern end of the village also ended with a cart track and later with the lifeboat house. A proper road was not built at that end until 1914 when the work was carried out by Prisoners of War.

Under the provision of the Local Government Act of 1894 the village was divided into two parts, Seaton and Seaton Carew, the latter forming the Seaton ward of the municipal borough of West Hartlepool. The division was the line from the Rocket House, through the middle of Front Street and along Church Street.

Early travelling was done by horseback, horse and cart or walking. By the late eighteenth century a better form of transport was required, especially to

James Lithgo sailing home in his coble, 1888. Pattison's Pictures

bring visitors from Darlington, so a regular coach service was begun. In 1783 the Darlington and Seaton Diligence was travelling every Tuesday and Thursday throughout the summer. The carriage carried three passengers inside at 3d a mile each. The poorer people travelled by stage wagon, a slow cart pulled by six to eight horses, with a carter walking alongside. The carts were also used for the transportation of goods. Parcels were carried by a cart man on certain days on payment of a fee. In 1828 Joseph Atkinson carried

A horse and cart turns into Church Street while another transports a little family along Front Street outside the Royal Cafe in 1888. Pattison's Pictures

The railway station in 1888. William Bosomworth, the Station Master chats to a commuter. Prior to 1883, when a new waiting room and other buildings were erected in red brick, the station was described as open and uncomfortable. The buildings have now gone and the platform is open once again. Pattison's Pictures

A tram rattling along Front Street, c1905. Author's Collection

parcels between Stockton and Seaton every Wednesday and Saturday. Robert Ferguson was the postman and he carried letters to Stockton at 6am every morning in the summer and Tuesday and Saturday in the winter. He returned to Seaton at noon. On 4 July 1836 White and Browns coach gave a regular service. The coach left Hartlepool at 7am four days a week. It went through Seaton at 8am on its way to Stockton and returned at 3pm. The fare from Seaton to Stockton was 2s. On 12 June 1837 John Brown began running

Looking south along Front Street with a tram at the end of the line. The lifeboat house in the distance marks the end of the village, c1905. Author's Collection

An early motor vehicle. This view of the shops and the bandstand was taken from the window of number 30 The Front, c1935. Author's Collection

the Stockton coach five days a week. It left Hartlepool at 8am and went by way of New Stranton reaching Seaton at 8.30am then through Greatham to Stockton. The cost was 3s (15p) inside and 2s 6d (13p) outside. Advertised as the only coach that ran throughout the year, it is not known whether its route was through Carr House and Cliff House farms or up Seaton Lane to Owton Manor Lane End and through Cauld Knuckles (near to where the Traveller's Rest now stands).

Paddle steamers and other sailing vessels were a popular form of transport for sightseers and were recorded from as early as 1813. From about 1831 trips would go from Hartlepool to Whitby, Newcastle, Middlesbrough and other destinations. In 1836 the railway linked the Hartlepool and Clarence lines with Seaton. To begin with the line was used mainly for the transportation of goods but eventually the railway became a popular form of transport for visitors. John Proctor, in conjunction with the railways, ran an omnibus from the station to the village. On Good Friday, 28 March 1902 a tram began to run from Church Street to Seaton. The line ran from Church Street, along Mainsforth Terrace and over Newburn Bridge. Between the end of the bridge and the beginning of the village the line was carried along the sea banks in the form of a light railway. The end of the tramline was the corner of Front and Church Street at the *Seaton Hotel*. The stop was nicknamed Kelly's Corner because of the congestion that was caused with passengers embarking and disembarking. The last tram to Seaton ran on 25 March 1927, after which trolley buses were used.

In the early twentieth century cars were still only available to the wealthy so the main form of transport was still horses. Soapboxes on pram wheels were used to collect the horse manure from the roads and then take it to sell to gardeners. Bicycles would be used to collect a couple of sacks of sea-coal to keep the home fires burning. It would have been a common sight to see a bicycle being pushed through the sand loaded with a couple of bags of the heavy, black, dripping mess. It was to be about 1918 before cars, charabancs and lorries became more popular than the horse and cart.

From the seventeenth century the area had many quaint place names of which only a few now survive. Some of these are: North Stenling, Fences, Admire Flatt, Crook Dike, Butterscroft, Mass Gate, Tythers Old Barn, Marle Pot, Great Southfield, Little Southfield, Maddeson's Farm, Warren Marsh, Bakehouse Garth, Pond Close, Loaning Close, Longfives, Cow Road Close, Longflatt Close, Wood's Garth, Common Houses, Forty Riggs, Blind Sykes, Town End Close, Seaton Moor, Salvin Flatt, Cauld Knuckles, Chapel Open and Corner's Court.

According to early maps The Cliff was once known simply as the Highway and then Marine Road. The Front was known as Front Street until the early twentieth century.

An aerial view taken in 1955. By 1960 the area would no longer look like a village as nearly all the fields in this view became housing estates. Courtesy of Simmons Aerofilms Ltd

Chapter Five

Occupations & Industries

Near to the mouth of the River Tees, on Greatham and Seaton marshes, there remain traces of ancient salt-works. These date from at least the fourteenth century and possibly earlier. Salt, to be used for the preservation of food, was made by an evaporation process from ancient times until the nineteenth century. These salt-pits or pans would have been valuable commodities passed down through families of wealthy landowners. From 1421 to 1439 it appears that there were at least four salt-pits in the manor of Seaton, one with the curious title of 'Make Beggar'. On 10 December 1586, William and Annie Barton leased their messuage and 'four bowles of salte' for twenty-one years to the Wood family. On 11 February 1888 the Seaton Carew Salt Boring Company found salt at a depth of 1,200 feet.

There is a deed dated 1691 that leases for 99 years *'coal mines within the manor of Seaton at a rent of 6s 8d per annum per pit'*. This indicates that either

Barefoot cockle women heading down to the rocks in 1888. Pattison's Pictures

Pattison's caption 'What are friends for?' Barefoot cockle women climbing up from the rocks in 1888. Pattison's Pictures

coal was mined within the area, which is highly unlikely, or this deed would have referred to the foreshore and sea-coal. There are also early records of salmon fisheries of which two still existed in the early nineteenth century.

Many of the men in the village would have more than one means of income, besides having a business, perhaps a shop; they might own one or more boats for fishing. In the late nineteenth century, when the railway became established, the fish would be packed in ice and sent to the larger cities. It would not

Pattison's caption 'A good catch'. Women checking their catch in1888. Pattison's Pictures

Mrs Hodgson selling her kippers to Mrs Stevenson and her daughter, Grace, at their house on Front Street in 1888. Pattison's Pictures

The one that didn't get away. A fish-seller in the back-yard of a house in 1888. Pattison's Pictures

be unusual to be in a London restaurant eating fish from the waters around Seaton. The women also did their share of work by mending nets, shrimping, smoking fish and selling their products door to door. Cockle women would eke out a living by climbing over the rocks in their bare feet to collect fresh shellfish. As Seaton became busy the fishermen used their boats for fishing trips or sightseeing tours for the visitors.

Sea-coal has been collected from the beach from the beginning of the nineteenth century and possibly earlier. The sea-coal rake was the arms of the village in the 1880s. To begin with the coal would have been for domestic use only, hawked from door to door to fill the coal-houses. As the larger industries developed the sea-coal became big business. In the 1960s there were about 200 vehicles working on the beach. The men would wait on the beach at high tide watching to see where the coal would be deposited. They would mark off their 'patch' and when the tide receded would rake the coal into piles and shovel it onto their vehicles. Once collected it would be deposited at yards where it was washed and then sold on. The coal would be crushed and mixed with open-cast coal to be used as pulverised fuel. Gradually the amount of coal being washed up declined and, by about 1985, the boom was over. The coal is still collected but in much smaller quantities. There are conflicting ideas on where this black gold comes from. One theory is that it came from the mines further up the coast. Coal and slate would be put on conveyor belts and once the large lumps of coal had been removed the rest would be dumped into the sea and would then be moved around by the tides. As the mines closed the

Children shrimping near the rocks on Seaton beach in 1888. Pattison's Pictures

Collecting sea-coal with a horse and cart in 1888. Pattison's Pictures

coal became rarer. Another theory is that it comes from the wrecked colliers. As the wood rotted under the sea the coal would spill out and, again, this would eventually diminish. The third possibility is that it comes from coal seams under the sea which divers tell us are there. The sea-coal that is found is of different quality and size so perhaps all three theories are correct.

Seal Sands, about a mile from the centre of the village, was named because of the hundreds of grey seals that lived and bred there. By the beginning of the twentieth century every seal had disappeared. This was attributed to the building of industry and pollution. One of the images from Pattison's Pictures shows

Pattison's caption 'Seaton at the North Pole,' a man draped in seal furs, to detract from his human scent, has returned from a seal cull and poses with his gun and 'kill' in 1888. Pattison's Pictures

Harvesting in Charlie Lamb's field in August 1889. Pattison's house can be seen in the background. Pattison's Pictures

that industry was not the only factor instrumental in the seals' decline; they were also killed by man. Seals were reintroduced in the area in the late twentieth century and are now breeding quite happily.

Until the middle of the twentieth century the village was surrounded by fertile farmland. The principal crops grown were wheat, oats, potatoes, barley and turnips. Many of the villagers would own one or more fields to supplement their income or to grow food for their horses.

Cliff House Pottery was opened in Mainsforth Terrace by William Smith in 1880. He took over some empty buildings that once housed an engineering factory. These stood a few hundred yards from Cliff House Farm. Smith employed mainly women and girls, of whom there were plenty in need of work. Employing over a hundred workers the pottery had some very productive years but due to rising costs and cheap imports it closed in 1897.

Large industries from the mid nineteenth century were to begin the change in the way the Seaton people earned their living. Cliff House Iron Works was established in 1858 by Samuel Bastow and used, amongst other equipment, for the manufacture of railway trucks and steam cranes. This was later taken over by William Gray. Seaton Carew Iron Company was the largest exporter in the UK of basic iron of the Thomas Gilchrist process of 1890. The company was eventually bought over by Dorman Long.

Reclamation of the land to be used for grazing livestock began in the early eighteenth century. By the 1890s vast amounts of the River Tees estuary had been reclaimed. Slag, which had previously been costly and

Robert Ferguson in his little cobbler's shop in Charles Street in 1888. Another shoemaker in the village at the same time was George Robinson. Pattison's Pictures

difficult to dispose of, was given free by the ironmasters and was used to construct walls to channel the River Tees to the required course. The river channel was dredged and the silt from the river-bed was used to reclaim the foreshore. Industry quickly took over this land. The Seaton Carew Zinc works became established in 1906. Houses, a school, clubhouse and shops were built for the workers and their families. There were also houseboats

Ben Jones cutting ribs of beef at Crosby's butchers on Front Street in 1888. Pattison's Pictures

moored to provide accommodation. The formula for the process used for the zinc came from Belgium so many of the workers were Belgian but the works also gave employment to the people of Seaton. A short time later sulphur works were built. William Gray purchased 100 acres of land near

From left to right Kitty Bill, Richard Tate 'Dick' Myers, Wilkinson and Alf Sewell standing in the doorway, of South End House in 1888. Pattison's Pictures

Dick Myers and nineteen year old Harry Ferguson outside South End House in 1888. Pattison's Pictures

Ralph, at age fifty-seven, and young Fred Noddings at Noddings and Elder's joinery shop in Charles Street in 1888. Pattison's Pictures

William Proctor, William Odgers and Ralph Noddings having a chat at Noddings and Elder's shop in 1888. Pattison's Pictures

Seaton and the land was developed in 1913. This was to become known as Graythorp. Gray established a shipyard with houses and facilities for the workers and their families. In 1929 Gray's had built its 1000th ship. Employing hundreds of workers, even through the slump of the 1930s, the site eventually closed in 1968. Laing's Offshore took over the site in 1972. Planning permission was granted for the Nuclear Power Station in 1967

Dunning and old George outside the brew-house in Ashburn Street in 1888. Pattison's Pictures

and the station opened in 1972. Chemical plants were built between Seaton and Redcar. Many of these industries are still in production although with fewer employees than in the early years.

Many other occupations were carried out in the village at the time Pattison was taking his pictures. The Parish Clerk and Sexton was William Odgers. William Bosomworth was stationmaster and Joshua Ervin and

The Seaton Cricket Team in 1888 at Forcett Park in Darlington. Pattison's Pictures

Robert Corner were signalmen. William Johnson, living in North Road, was the village policeman. In Church Street William Proctor was the insurance agent for Phoenix Fire and a cab proprietor, Harry Tilly, a solicitor, Isabella Hall ran a drapers and James Dodd was a cart owner. In Charles Street Robert Ferguson had a cobbler's shop, Robert Corner was a cart owner and Ralph Noddings and his son ran Noddings and Elder's Joinery shop. On Front Street there was a post office combined with a grocery shop run by the postmaster, William Kidson. Letters arrived at 8 am and 6.30 pm and were dispatched at 6.35 pm and 10.50 pm. On Front Street Lazarus Bowser and Jane Vitty also had grocery shops, John Crosby, George Hindson and Robert Ramsey were all butchers, George and Michael Dixon, tailors, William Sewell, a fruiterer, Samuel Biggart MD, a doctor and William Weastell was a cooper. Christopher Bell had his blacksmith's shop at South End House and James Robson, also a blacksmith, was on Ashburn Street. Joseph Peacock had a grocer's shop on the Green and there was also Richard Burton, a bricklayer, Charles Lamb, a farmer and carting contractor and David Churnside, a gardener. Lodging houses were run by Mrs Hannah Woodward, Mrs Margaret Robinson, Mrs Mary Ann Lamb, Mrs Elizabeth Crawford, Mrs Elizabeth Marriner and Miss Mary Ann Lithgow. Mrs Ann Bell was a laundress, Emily Burton, a rate collector, the Maunder Brothers, florists, James Marshall and Ramsey and Gilchrist, brewers and there were also numerous farmers and pilots. Robert Chilton was the low lighthouse keeper until George Emerson succeeded him.

Chapter Six

Religious Buildings

6.1 Seaton Chapel

Records show that there was once a chapel in the village. Historians agree that the chapel was dedicated to Thomas a' Beckett. Thomas of Canterbury died in 1170 but was not canonised until 1172 so the chapel must have been built after that date. In 1189 Peter de Carrowe held a knight's fee in Seton and Oueton. In 1200 Roald, Prior of Guisbrough, granted to Walter, son of Peter Lord of Seton-Carrow, a perpetual chantry within the Chapel of Seaton. The churches of Stranton and Hart along with their respective chapels of Hartlepool and Seaton were given to the Guisbrough Priory by de Brus. Seaton did not share the fate of the other de Brus properties when they lost their estates in 1306. A document survives showing that the

All Saint's Church in Stranton in 1888. The villagers used this church and churchyard until Holy Trinity was built in 1831. Pattison's Pictures

chapel was still attached to Guisbrough Priory in 1311 and was serviced by a canon from the priory until the Dissolution of the Monasteries, which was between 1536 and 1540. In 1315 Prior Geoffrey determined that the Vicar of Stranton was bound to provide for the maintenance of Seaton Chapel. From 1577 to 1588 the chapel was served by a stipendiary priest.

By 1622 the chapel was in ruins. Its exact location had never been determined, but in the late nineteenth century local tradition pointed to a site halfway down Seaton Snook 'where the old hermit dwelt' and where, in 1885, stonework foundation had been discovered. It was said by the lighthouse keeper of that year that locals and antiquarians thought it possible that a barn built by a Mr Pearse stood on the site and was partially constructed with stone from the old chapel. On the Admiralty Charts there is a gap in the sandbanks marked as Chapel Entry. Wherever the chapel once stood there is no trace left. In the early centuries communities usually sprang up in close proximity to their places of worship so it is likely there was an earlier Seaton village, now also long gone.

At a time when Seaton did not have its own church it was in the parish of Stranton. The villagers attended All Saint's Church and were buried in the churchyard there. The funeral bier would be carried along the White Dyke to Stranton. Eventually a hearse was built by Willie Walker which had two cart wheels in front to make it easier for the pall bearers.

6.2 Holy Trinity Church

Lady Barbara Isabella Lawson of the West Riding of Yorkshire bought land in Seaton at a cost of £300. These were the days when 'commissioner' churches were being built at a very fast pace to keep up with the ever

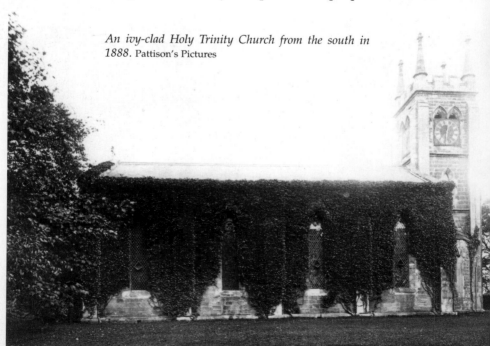

An ivy-clad Holy Trinity Church from the south in 1888. Pattison's Pictures

A view looking along Church Street to the church from Front Street in 1888. Pattison's Pictures

The interior of Holy Trinity Church before the chancel was raised in 1889. Pattison's Pictures

Holy Trinity churchyard in 1890. John Lawson's grave is the large plot to the right of the image. Pattison's Pictures

growing population. The church, much smaller than it is today, was designed by Thomas Pickersgill and was built in 1831 on Lady Lawson's land at a cost of about £1,700. On 29 September of the same year the church was consecrated by William Van Mildert, the last of the Prince Bishops of Durham. Built in stone with a south port, nave and a square western tower with pinnacles and a clock, it had seating for about 260 people. In 1842 the chancel, gallery and sanctuary, designed by the architect Jackson, were added. These additions meant there was now seating for 510 people. A new organ costing £50, built by Joseph Walker of London, was paid for by John Lawson. In 1864 the interior of the church was rearranged and open benches were installed at a cost of £425. In 1891 the chancel was raised and re-roofed, the organ chamber and vestry were added, a new organ was built, new heating installed and the nave re-floored. The total cost for the work was £800. In February 1921 four bells and a clock were installed in the tower.

The interior of the church hosts some beautiful stained glass and brass-work which has been given by patrons in memory of their loved ones. Some of the woodwork is also of the finest quality, made by Robert Thompson of Kilburn, the 'Mouseman,' so called because of his trademark consisting of a tiny carved mouse on his work.

Burials still took place at Stranton until 1842 when part of the Holy Trinity's church ground was consecrated. Further sections were consecrated in 1866 and 1908. More than 2000 souls are now buried in

The vicarage, with the church tower peeping out above the trees and sheep grazing peacefully on what is now the school field in 1888. Pattison's Pictures

Holy Trinity Churchyard. One of the gravestones is fashioned as a cross with an anchor and chain entwined in stone. This was erected and dedicated in 1873 by John Lawson and the villagers of Seaton in memory of unknown sailors. The epitaph, which is now almost obliterated by weathering, reads:

> *Around this same stone lie the remains of sailors who perished in the mighty waters and whose bodies were washed on shore from the wrecked vessels. Dedicated by the villagers. Be ye also ready.*

A lady who was a regular summer visitor to Seaton wrote a touching poem in 1879:

> *Oh calm they lay here side by side, the silent sleeping forms*
> *Cast up mid tangle and mid shell by our fierce northern storms.*
> *Husbands, fathers, brothers, sons, what hearts are breaking yet*
> *For those who rest here past away from loss and care and fret?*
> *What homes their dearest welcomes keep, their closest fondness saves?*
> *What desperate love still waits for them*
> *In Seaton's nameless graves?*

Another gravestone marks the final resting place for two sailors from Finland. Their bodies were washed onto Seaton beach after their ship, the *Birger*, was wrecked at Redcar in 1898. There are many recorded burials in the parish register between 1851 and 1900 of men and boys washed up on the beach with the word 'unknown' in place of a name. It is believed that altogether there could have been as many as 200 nameless burials in Holy Trinity Churchyard. During the German raids two Zeppelin pilots were

The vicarage in 1888, showing the extensive gardens. Pattison's Pictures

The vicarage in the early twentieth century. Author's Collection

The dining room of the vicarage in 1888. Pattison's Pictures

shot down and buried in a corner of the churchyard. In 1962 their remains were moved to a war cemetery at Cannock Chase.

The vicarage was designed by Anthony Salvin and built in 1837. The locals who remember the formidable, ivy covered structure thought it an

Sarah Swainson's wedding party in the garden of the vicarage in July 1890. Pattison's Pictures

eerie building. Sadly, in the 1970s, before conservation laws were put in place, because of its upkeep and cost of repair, the vicarage was demolished. A little piece of Seaton's history wiped out because of the lack of finances.

Lady Lawson's two sons, James and John, had been newly ordained at St Alban Hall at Oxford University. James became the first clergyman to Seaton parish remaining until 1833 before moving to another diocese. He was succeeded by Reverend Arthur Guiness. John Lawson took over the parish in 1835 and was to remain a much loved vicar until his death. He was buried on 10 August 1890 in the graveyard beside the church he had served for fifty-five years. The Reverend left a son, also John, and a daughter, Margaret. The clergy that followed from 1890 were:

Vicars

Francis WPJ Mortimer	1890–1894	Charles BR Hunter	1894–1909
Charles F Bickmore	1909–1917	Frederick B Beaven	1917–1927
George Robinson Cook	1927–1932	F Oswald Scott	1933–1935
James Booth	1936–1954	Joseph Maughan	1955–1962
Cecil Charles Greenwood	1962–1972	John Edward Scott	1973–1974
William Worley	1976–2003		

Curates

James Benjamin Baynard	1875–1876	Reginald Robson	1932–1935
James Whitehead Pattison	1885–1890	Herbert P. Johnson	1957–1961
Ernest Malcolm Sidebottom	1954–1956		
Frederick GJ Robinson	1881–1885		

A correspondent for the *London Times* passed through Seaton in 1869. He was to later write: *'The church was almost hidden in ivy and looked more venerable than a church three times its age, and within hand shaking distance stands the parsonage'.*

6.3 Quaker Chapel

Seaton would not have developed in the way that it did had it not been for the wealthy Darlington Quakers, most of whom were connected with banking. Throughout the late eighteenth and most of the nineteenth century the village was their seaside retreat. Some of them bought houses in the village to use in the summer months. Names such as Pease, Mounsey and Backhouse were associated with Seaton throughout the years. In 1841 a little white chapel was built by the Quakers to hold their meetings in the summer months. As places further afield became more accessible with modern travel the Quaker element moved on and the chapel was sold to William Lithgo. For a time it was used for dances and other functions, then became a laundry. It ended its life being used by the gardening club as storage for tools and manure before finally being demolished in the 1960s.

The Quaker Chapel once used every summer by its founders. Here it reaches the end of its life. Courtesy of George Colley

6.4 Wesleyan Chapel

The first chapel seated about 100 people and was erected in 1830 on Front Street when Hartlepool and Seaton belonged to the Wesleyan circuit. In stormy weather the person delivering the sermon would have to compete with the roar of the ocean while sea spray would spatter the chapel windows. In the 1870s it was decided that the chapel was inadequate for public worship so it was rebuilt. On Tuesday, 10 September 1878 Arthur Pease of Darlington laid the foundation stone. A bottle containing copies of the *South Durham Herald*, the *Northern Evening Mail* and the *Weekly Methodist* was placed under the stone. The new chapel opened on 13 November 1878. The building was much larger than the previous one with seating now for 200 people. The work was completed at a total cost of £300 which had been raised by donation, due largely to the energies of Mr Lancelot Middleton. Some of the funding came from the Society of Friends and from Reverend Lawson's efforts. In 1932 the Primitive Methodist, Wesleyan and United Methodists combined to form one church. In the early twentieth century the chapel closed for services and was used as a bingo hall. An amusement arcade now stands on the site. It is highly likely that the side and rear walls that once belonged to the chapel still remain as part of the arcade. As far as it is known, the bottle containing the 1878 news of the day still remains under the foundations. The Methodist Church in Station Lane opened in 1912.

A view in 1888 looking over the old cannon to the Wesleyan Chapel on Front Street. The barometer, which was painted yellow at this time, can be seen on the footpath to the left of the image. Pattison's Pictures

The title 'Wesleyan' became 'Methodist' because it was thought by the students of the founder of the faith, John Wesley, that the rules were strict and methodical. Wesley visited Hartlepool on six occasions in the years 1757, 1759, 1761, 1766, 1784 and 1786. On one of his visits he stayed at a cottage in Seaton. North-west of Seaton Green stood Bath House and a cottage adjoining which had belonged to James Lithgo, who had been the custom house manager. The cottage had been a public house 100 years previously, the landlord at that time being Bartle Dowell. At the time of Wesley's visit the occupier was Mr E Ellinor, a seaman of more than fifty years. He was the owner of a brig called the *Thomas and Mary* which traded to Holland. Mr Ellinor made a pulpit out of old ships' wood to be placed in the kitchen of the cottage from where John Wesley would preach his sermons to a small congregation. Mr Ellinor died at the age of 96 and was buried in Stranton Churchyard. John Wesley died in March 1791.

Chapter Seven

Inns & Hotels

7.1 The Ship & the New Inn

In 1791 George Pearson, a gentleman of Durham, had property in Seaton. By 1792 he had ownership in a salmon fishery and he bought a considerable estate from the assignees of Robert Preston of Stockton. This estate included the *Ship Inn,* which had belonged to Robert Johnson and Watson, with stables, coach houses, gardens and a bowling green; two freehold fields near to the inn comprising sixteen acres; three cattlegates in the Snook; a freehold house and farm called Hunter House Farm; several freehold closes containing 262 acres with thirty-four pasture gates; two houses and two farms; six closes containing fifty-five acres with two leasehold closes and ten pasture gates; six closes containing eighty-five acres; two closes containing thirteen acres with a dwelling house and three pasture gates; all in Seaton Carew; with tithes of corn and grain. In May 1794 a pre-nuptial settlement of the estate was agreed between George Pearson, Ralph Ord and William Chaytor when Pearson was to marry Chaytor's daughter, Betty. She was left a widow by 1804. The Pearson's

Looking down Church Street from Front Street in 1888, with the Seaton Hotel on the left of the image. A sign for billiards can be seen on the wall. Pattison's Pictures

The Seaton Hotel in 1902. Mr Hodgson's name was above the door at this time stating that he was the landlord. Author's Collection

only daughter, who married George Hutton Wilkinson, a barrister from Harperly, became sole heir.

Very soon after Pearson bought the estate he pulled down the old inn and, on the site, built a coach house with six adjoining lodging houses to cater for the influx of Quaker visitors. These buildings were erected using dressed limestone and Westmoreland slate roofs and the hotel was fitted with Venetian windows. One kitchen served the both the coach house and the six lodging houses. The cellars had a passageway connecting all the buildings via the kitchen. There was also a wooden balcony that the guests used to go from the hotel to their lodgings. The second floor room that faces the sea was originally a ballroom with a gallery for a small orchestra. Outside were two portico walks, one above the other, the second raised to roof height enabling guests to shelter from the rain whilst admiring the magnificent view. As well as gardens there were stables for the horses and accommodation for the grooms and servants. Pearson called the hotel the *New Inn* but the title was changed over the years and eventually became the *Seaton Hotel*. The hotel must have been sold after Pearson's death but his son-in law, George Wilkinson, still held the deeds to at least two of the lodging houses. One was leased to a tenant by Wilkinson in 1849 and

Church Street in 1888, looking towards the sea, showing the lodging houses on the right that were built with the Seaton Hotel in 1792. Pattison's Pictures

another, 'Kirklea,' was sold to Reverend Lawson in June 1843.

In 1796 an advertisement was placed by the proprietor of the hotel that read as follows:

> *Alexander Goalbraith returns his most grateful thanks for past favours and takes the liberty of acquainting them and the public in general, that he still continues at the New Inn at Seaton Carew, has taken the several elegant lodging houses and fitted them up in the most genteel & comfortable manner, so as to be admirably well suited for the accommodation of private families or single persons. He had laid in a stock of neat wines & other liquors of the best quality. This Inn contains a well proportioned & very elegant long-room 15 feet high, sitting rooms, commodious bedchambers & a modern built hot bath with a convenient dressing-room adjoining. There are also promenades & pleasant walks, which as well as the Inn & other houses, have a much fuller command than any other part of the coast, of these delightful land & sea prospects for which the neighbourhood of Hartlepool has ever been so much & justly admired. The beach at Seaton is 5 miles in length & of great breadth at low water, perfectly firm & smooth. In short, there is not perhaps in this island, at least in the North, a place so well calculated for enjoying all the comforts & delights resulting from sea-bathing at Seaton Carew. The bathing machines are moved with the utmost facility to any depth that may be*

The two houses that were built in 1792 with the Seaton Hotel that stood where the entrance to the car park is now. The next building along the row with the bay windows is Durham House, c1910. Author's Collection

required. There is a regular post established from Stockton, & a carrier every day in the season. Mr Goalbraith has engaged proper cooks, waiters &c. & flatters himself, that by his earnest & unremitting endeavours to give satisfaction (his board & lodgings being on the most reasonable terms) he shall merit the approbation of those who may be pleased to honour him with their company.

After Mr Goalbraith's demise, his wife continued running the business. In William Tate's little book about Seaton, Stranton and Hartlepool in 1812 he wrote:

A woman in every way adequate to such an undertaking, her engaging manner, even deportment and unwearied assiduity to oblige each rank and station, gain the favour and esteem of everyone. All domestic business is carried out with the greatest order and regularity under her own immediate inspection. There is an ordinary every day throughout the bathing season, and the tables are plentifully supplied with good and honest fare. Parties from Hartlepool, Redcar and Coatham, in their water excursions, frequently dine or take their tea here.

Mrs Goalbraith was again mentioned in the *Durham Chronicle* on 3 February 1815 where there was a report on the Hartlepool fishermen going to the rescue of the crew of the *Betsy* which was wrecked on Longscar in January of that year. The crew of nine was saved from certain death. The report read; *'the sailors were hospitably entertained by Mrs Goalbraith, who procured every refreshment for them, of which they stood so much in need'*.

Other proprietors from 1827 were: Robert Proctor, Christopher Harbron, Thomas White, George Emerson and William and Dorothy Bond. For a few years prior to 1855 the hotel had been called *Murrays*. After 1855 the proprietors were Mr Ramsey, John Bird and Mrs Sothren. On 13 December 1869, Joseph Barker Hodgson, a brewer, acquired the hotel with its paddock and garden. By this time the lodging houses had been sold off separately and where the kitchen had been was now an archway to the stables. In 1869 a newspaper report stated:

The old visitors were falling away. A generation before the visitors were quality, the dandies dressed in pantaloons and claw-hammer tailed coats, the ladies dressed in plain bands, short skirts and sandaled shoes. Now the pitman turned jobber and the navvy turned contractor are the present 'quality'. The previous generation remembers when the Seaton Hotel's stables were full and the attached lodging houses were approached by a wooden balcony, which is now in a state of disrepair.

In January 1870 a ball took place under the watchful eye of Mrs Sothren, who remained as proprietor until later that year. The ball was attended by a small but very select company who danced until the early hours of the morning. Hodgson died in 1870 and the hotel was sold to Mr Harry Thornton 'a proper Yorkshire tyke' who completely transformed the building. Mrs Thornton's culinary expertise was of widespread fame. In 1871 Mr Thornton placed an advertisement in the *South Durham Herald* which read:

Splendid sands, capital sea-bathing, hot water salt baths, bracing climate and excellent lodgings at the Seaton Hotel, which has been newly decorated and furnished. Cabs, carriages and saddle horses; billiards &c. Seaton Carew is about ten miles from Stockton-on-Tees and two miles from West Hartlepool. The railway station is about two minute's walk of the village. Cabs meet every train.
*　　Henry Thornton, proprietor, late of Middlesbrough and York.*

Three years later, on 15 August 1874, another advertisement appeared showing that the Thornton's enterprise was short-lived:

On Tuesday 11th, the valuable property known as the Seaton Hotel, and at present in the occupation of the late Mr Thornton's representatives, was offered by Mr Flavell, on the premises for sale by auction. The highest bid was £1900 and the auction was concluded because the reserve price of £2100 was not met.

A few days later the hotel was bought by Mr Moffat, an innkeeper from Middlesbrough, for £2000. The *Seven Stars Inn* had also been up for auction that day but was not sold. From 1885 to 1902 the proprietors of the *Seaton Hotel* were Charles Haylock, Miss Anne Thornton, Emily Thornton and Mr Hodgson. From 1902 to 1908 the hotel was owned by J Henderson and Sons and managed by Mrs GT Reay, S Swain, GP Thompson and from 1920 to 1924 Peter G Hodgson. The hotel was bought by Nimmos in the late 1920s and Whitbread took over in 1963. Some of the tenants and managers from the twentieth century to the present are: WC Brown, A Jackson, Bert Reevley, George Lacey, Syd and Gladys Cartman, Bob Calvert, Jimmy Eccles, 1971 to 1984 Jackie and Madge McClean, 1993 to 1998 Kevin and Denise Jones, John and Diane Chrystal, Roy and Marie Grantham and John Clarke.

The hotel is reputed to have a resident ghost who has scared staff and residents on many occasions. There have certainly been unexplained noises, incidents and a feeling of a room becoming very cold. A baby has also been heard crying. No! It's not the whisky! Young people and teetotallers have reported strange goings-on. The story is, whether legend or fact, that a coachman's wife was murdered in the old *Ship Inn* and she has remained on the site searching for her baby. When repairs were being carried out in the cellar an opening was found that was believed to have once been a tunnel to the beach. This could have been for pipes and a pump to bring in the salt water for the baths or it may have been for drainage purposes. At one time all of the village sewerage was pumped straight into the sea. Where the stables were at the rear of the building, at some point in time, they were knocked down and small garages put in their place. In the 1960s these garages were demolished and a tunnel was found that

Kirklea, now number 7 Church Street. Built as one of the lodging houses attached to the Seaton Hotel in 1792. The small part of a building that can be seen on the right was demolished to make room for a driveway. It is thought it was once used as a blacksmith's shop, c1900. Courtesy of Steve Frain

must have been under the original stables. It was thought that it once lead to the churchyard. Perhaps it was for smugglers or wreckers to escape with their loot!

7.2 The Seven Stars & the Marine

The *Seven Stars* would have either been built after Pearson's inn or, more likely, would have been established in a converted cottage of earlier date. Prior to the eighteenth century, when the Quakers began to use Seaton as their resort, there would have only been enough custom for one public house in the village. By the beginning of the nineteenth century there would have been the need for more than one. The Quakers abstained from alcohol so would not frequent the more bawdy public houses. By 1812 there were still only 50 or 60 houses in Seaton but many of them, by then, took paying guests. Up until 1820 the *Seven Stars* was run by Mrs Corner. '*A very judicious and obliging hostess who has long been well supported by a great many respectable people*'. Mrs Corner's son took over from her and was still there until 1852. He was followed by Mr George Good who, as well as running the inn and brewing his own ale, had a license to rent out hack horses. When he retired a widow took over and the small inn

The Seven Stars with the sign above the door stating 'Good's Seven Stars Hotel'. The building was demolished in 1900 to make way for the Marine Hotel, c1885. Author's Collection

The Marine Hotel in about 1905. The large ivy covered Ashburn House adjoining was demolished in 1923 to make way for a hotel car park. Courtesy of George Colley

became very dilapidated in her hands. George Good then came out of retirement and returned to the inn in about 1860 and spruced it up until it became a comfortable hostelry once more. He continued as landlord throughout the 1870s. His daughter, Elizabeth Hayes Good, took over from about 1885 until the inn closed in 1900. In that year the *Seven Stars*

The cannons and bandstand in front of the Marine Hotel. The cannons were removed to be used for scrap in 1937, c1925. Author's Collection

was demolished and the *Marine Hotel* was built on the site. The new hotel was described as;

> *A large and handsome structure; it is arranged so as to meet the convenience of families, commercial travellers and visitors, is lighted throughout by electricity and contains billiard, drawing and dining rooms.*

In 1923 Ashburn House, which belonged to the Mounsey family, on the adjoining plot to the *Marine Hotel* was demolished to make way for a car park to service the hotel. From 1916 to 1918 the hotel was taken over by the RAF to billet the personnel that were based at the Seaton Carew airfields. Camerons then bought the hotel and some of their managers until the early 1960s were: AH Eve, Mrs RM Graham, AF Emmerson, Miss E Clough and H Atkinson. Between the 1960s and 1980s Dick and Monica Taylor followed by Joe and Shirley Brown ran the establishment. Camerons eventually sold the property and for the past few years until the present the hotel has been owned and run by Lee and Claire Dexter.

7.3 The King's Head Inn:

In 1803 Robert Henry McDonald built the *King's Head Inn* on the west side of the Green. In 1812 the landlord was William Oliver and in 1827 William Webster. From 1851 to 1861 the landlady was Margaret Walker. Between

Seaton Hall in 1886, built as the King's Head in 1803, William Thomlinson bought the building in 1882 and lived there until his death in 1943. Author's Collection.

1862 and 1872 the inn was bought by JW Richardson who completely transformed the building and grounds. The stables and coach houses were converted into summer houses for the guests and vineyards and croquet grounds were laid out. William Thomlinson bought the *King's Head* in 1882 and, renaming it Sea View House, converted the building into a private residence. The house later became known as Seaton Hall. The large attic room is panelled in louvred sections of wood with semi circular oak plinths separating each section. The timber is known to have come from a ship that foundered at Seaton. It is thought that the ship was a German vessel the *Krokodil* or *Crocodile*. To the rear of the building part of the large secluded courtyard still remains with some of its cobbled paths still intact. When Lawson Road was still a dirt track there was a gate leading from the courtyard to an orchard. The old *King's Head* eventually catered for guests once again when it was bought by Mr Hugill and became the *Seaton Hall Hotel*. The building is now the Seaton Hall Nursing Home.

7.4 The George & Dragon Inn

Very few surviving records can be found on the second inn which stood on the Green so it is not known exactly when it was built. It was named the *George and Dragon* and there is mention of it in 1812. The landlords were Mr and Mrs Robert Harbron and it was said that a large clientele of gentlemen farmers and respectable tradesman along with their families used the hotel. Two documents survive dated 1 January 1831 with the heading *George and Dragon* and signed Rob Harbron. They are a bill and

The large building on the extreme right of the image on the north-east corner of the Green started life as the George and Dragon Inn, 1888. Pattison's Pictures

receipt for payment of 19s 5d (almost £1) for gin, rum, ale, cheese and bread consumed by the lifeboat crew on 12 December 1830. The crew went to the assistance of the *King Lear* and an unknown brig that were both wrecked on Longscar that day with the loss of all hands. Thomas Harbron, Robert's son, became landlord after his father. Between 1860 and 1870 the building was split into two dwellings with one being bought by Mr Cooper. One of the buildings is now the *Norton Hotel* and the other a private residence.

7.5 Staincliffe House

What is now the *Staincliffe Hotel* was built in 1869 as a residence by Thomas Walker. He was a wealthy West Hartlepool merchant employing 200 men at his sawmills in Mainsforth Terrace that had been established in 1851. Staincliffe House was built in a mixture of architectural styles. There were mullioned windows, open balustrades, towers and a cupola. When the house was built it was suggested that the building might *'soon become an island home with vast water privileges'*. If the banks and cliffs had not been reclaimed and consolidated the sea may well have swallowed up the north end of the village. Walker had a huge wall built around the house, perhaps

Staincliffe House in 1888, the private residence of Thomas Walker, later to become the Staincliffe Hotel. To the left of the main building the conservatory can be seen and to the right the Staincliffe Villas. Pattison's Pictures

A view of Staincliffe House in 1888 from the south with the chapel to the left of the building. Note the woman with a perambulator on the beach. Pattison's Pictures

to try to keep the sea from claiming the land. His house had lawns and kitchen gardens outside. A large conservatory adjoined the main building and there was a small, family chapel towards the south of his land. Shortly after he built his house Walker added six villas alongside. Walker had three daughters, Mabel, Mary and Maude, who was an artist and did some

A tennis party in August of 1889 at the courts to the north of Staincliffe House. Pattison's Pictures

lovely early sketches of Seaton. William Gray acquired the house and in 1921 presented it to his workforce to be used as Gray Convalescent Home. By 1929 the building had been bought to be used as a hotel but it was not licensed to sell alcohol until after 1938. The conservatory was removed and a large ballroom, with a sprung floor, built in its place. A second floor was added and, in a wonderful feat of engineering by TW Stonehouse, the whole roof was lifted off and replaced when the second floor was built.

7.6 Station Hotel

The *New Station Hotel* was built in about 1872 at the side of the footpath leading to the village. Adjoining the hotel was a cottage built by a very old resident who was a friend and patron of Ralph Ward Jackson. The cottage was eventually occupied by the Station Master. The hotel was described as *'A modern built building with a fashionable portico entrance, but rather built before its time'*. By this time the railways were being used by trippers and the hotel would have been a convenient stop-off point for a quick jar before the arrival of one's train. The hotel's first landlord was Mr Michael Bell who had previously been the stationmaster for Seaton Carew railway station. Other landlords that followed from 1890 were: Charles Haylock, T Dodds, from 1902 to 1929 Henry Musgrove and in the 1930s William Pybus Davey.

Pattison's caption 'Whip behind'. Bob Proctor with his cab at the Station Hotel in 1888. His young hitch-hiker seems to have bumped his head as he fell off the kickboard. Pattison's Pictures

As Bob waves his whip at the disembarked passenger, the boy still holding his seat appears to be trying to keep out of sight. The small building adjoining the hotel belonged to an old Seaton resident and was built before the adjoining hotel. It became the Station Master's house for a few years but has now been demolished, 1888. Pattison's Pictures

The village also had a small public house or beer-house, which was situated to the south of and on the same side as the *Seaton Hotel* towards the Snook. This was originally kept by Willy Ramsey. Thomas Wilkinson Watson was his successor then Hudson and, in 1873, the widow who had run the *Seven Stars*. There was a beer-house adjoining the *Seaton Hotel* kept by Mr TW Wilson. From at least 1873 there was a brew-house in Ashburn Street kept by Ramsey, Gilchrist and Ramsey. J Dunning was the drayman.

Chapter Eight

Past & Present Buildings

The oldest lived-in dwelling in Cleveland, according to the county archaeologist, is 7–9 Green Terrace. This was a cottage that had been empty for some time and was in such a bad state of repair the council had put a closing order on the building. Had it not been sold at that time it would have been demolished. Mr and Mrs Christison bought the old cottage and, in a labour of love, proceeded to make it not only habitable but absolutely charming and full of character. The project took more than four years to complete. The couple used as much of the original material as they possibly could. On the site they found fragments of pottery and they were passed to an archaeologist to date. Soon after the county archaeologist visited the property and told them that the fragments dated the original construction of the building to the fourteenth century, the medieval period. The cottage had extensions built at both ends in the seventeenth century. When a bomb exploded nearby during the Second World War part of the roof of the building collapsed exposing a seventeenth century dividing wall. Inside the cottage there is a recess in

Number 7 to 9 Green Terrace in 2000, a restored cottage dating from the medieval period said to be the oldest lived-in dwelling in Cleveland. The Author.

Tucked into the north-west corner of the Green is the house that was built in the Swiss style in 1834 by Robert Dixon. Haraap and Sterndale's school was situated in the large buildings on the right, 1888. Pattison's Pictures

Jim Drake with his horse and dog outside the large house on the corner of the Green and Green Terrace in 1888. The house was occupied by Mrs Margaret Robinson who took in paying guests. Pattison's Pictures

Children outside the National School in Ashburn Street in 1888. Pattison's Pictures

The golf clubhouse and lifeboat house from the Snook in 1888. The building behind the clubhouse is the buoy-house. Pattison's Pictures

J Simpson and S Hogg posing in front of the Staincliffe Villas with the Seaton lowlight to the right of the image, 1888. Pattison's Pictures

the wall of what is now used as a sitting room. This recess was one of the medieval doorways. The old doorway had a curve where the frame was worn smooth. It is possible that this would have been the entrance used to bring cattle in at night, their hides wearing the frame down. A large truss had been used as a roof support and when it was removed it was found to be the oak ribs of a sailing vessel. There was a type of ladder leading from the ground floor to the large loft. Both in a medieval and a seventeenth century farmhouse the sleeping quarters would have been above with the livestock below.

The Green, or Seaton Green as it was known, belonged to all the freeholders of Seaton. Three sides of the square still boast some very old and charming buildings dating from the early eighteenth to the late nineteenth century. At one time the houses formed a square and at the close of the eighteenth century William Hutchinson wrote:

The remains of the village of Seaton which have hithero escaped the encroachments of the ocean consist of a green, inclosed on three sides with cottages in the form of a square, and a row of houses stretching to the southward along the very brink of the sea-banks.

Station Lane with the twin peaked Gables and Ivycroft next door in1888. The former is now a nursing home and the latter Seaton Carew Social Club. Pattison's Pictures

Station Lane in 1888 showing Boddy's Farmhouse where the library is now situated. Pattison's Pictures

Franklin's corner viewed from the south in 1888, with the little cabman's shelter in the centre of the view. Pattison's Pictures

A view of children on the steps to the beach just north of Franklin's Corner in 1888. Pattison's Pictures

Children peering into a shop window somewhere in Seaton in 1888. Does anyone know where this shop was? Pattison's Pictures

In 1885 Robert Chilton, the oldest resident of the village, was asked what had become of the houses. He said that the high ground and the small cliff were washed away and the tide flowed over the houses. The houses were flooded and the occupants prudently retired, building their houses further inshore and yielding to the sea their disputed empire, *'Old Neptune removed them'*. It was reported that the houses were 'wretched hovels' so were no loss. There is a record that states that on *'3rd January, 1767 a great fall of snow, thunder and lightning for two days between Blyth and Whitby. At Seaton several houses were washed down'*. It is very likely that these were the fourth row of houses on the Green. It was also recorded that the deeds to some of these vanished properties were used by the owners to obtain money.

On the south side of the Green three cottages, now 14, 15 and 16, were two dwellings. There are indentures and wills relating to the properties dating from 1742. In 1811 these properties, amongst others, belonged to the Pattison family. In 1896 most of the property had been sold except for a small portion to the rear of Victoria Street which was retained by their heirs through marriage, the Paverly's. This land was also sold in 1920. In the north-west corner of the Green is a large house looking rather out of keeping with its neighbours. The date above the door is 1834 but parts of the rear and side of the building date back to 1792. The later part of the house was built by a magistrate, Robert William Dixon, designing the frontage to represent a Swiss chalet. Robert's father, James Henry McDonald Dixon JP, inherited Robert Henry McDonald's estates when he died in July 1838 without heir. The rest of the Green is comprised

Ambrose Storer's fancy goods and provision shop in about 1903. This is now number 30 and 31 The Front. Author's Collection

The Royal Café and the rocket house on the slipway to a very busy beach in 1913. As its name implies the Rocket House was used to store the firing mechanism that was used to attach ropes to distressed vessels. Author's Collection

of tall houses and cottages that date through to the nineteenth century. Many of the cottages were shops at one time, the last one closing in the late twentieth century.

On the slipway that leads to the beach opposite Church Street is a tiny little building on the left hand side. This was the Rocket House where the apparatus was kept for the rescue of vessels in distress. The building now serves as a part-time police station. Along Front Street (soon to change to The Front) large houses were built, mainly in the mid nineteenth century, and occupied by merchants and tradesmen. Many of these have either been demolished to make way for amusement arcades or the lower floors converted to shops. When alterations were being done to the rear of 30 and 31, The Front, in 1997, a huge well was found which would probably have served the whole row.

Part of South End curved away from the main road and at one end of the curve was the old Lifeboat House that was built in 1809 and may have been used to store equipment for the early lifeboats in a large storage area that was situated on the ground floor at the front of the building.

The two cottages to the north were built about 1770, one was South End House, now Anvil Cottage, and was Christopher 'Kitty Bill' Bell's blacksmith's shop for many years. There was also a blacksmith's shop near to the church worked by James Robson. Dick Myers, Henry Storer and Thomas Harrison were also blacksmiths in the village in the late nineteenth century. The other cottage may have belonged to a fisherman because the living accommodation was originally upstairs with the ground floor a large storage area. From the roof large iron hooks were suspended, probably to hang ropes and nets. The two large houses next door were one dwelling and probably pre-date the cottages. It is believed

Built on the corner of The Cliff and Station Lane in 1900, this was the premises of LS Thompson and housed a café and smoke room later to become Shingfield's Groceries and Provisions. Courtesy of George Colley

that the house was used by Lord John Eldon as a holiday home in the summer months. Ancient cottages along the main road on the south of the village were demolished in 1974. What is now the Royal Café is believed to have been built in the early part of the 1790s as a farmhouse. The occupiers could have looked out of their windows and watched their cattle and sheep grazing on the Snook.

Many small schools existed in the eighteenth and early nineteenth centuries. Often lessons would be taught in rooms rented from the parish authorities or in private dwellings. The teacher was usually 'a dame,' an older woman needing a means of support and having some sort of general knowledge of the fundamentals of reading and writing. Pupils would often have to take their own 'crackets' (stools) to sit on.

Lord Crewe of Stene in Northamptonshire, who was a descendant of the Bishop of Durham, Nathaniel Crewe, left £5 a year to Seaton for a school to be set up and maintained. The first school was believed to have been situated in a one storey, whitewashed building on The Cliff near to the Green beyond, what was then, Tudor Terrace. A solicitor, Mr Dodd had erected the building. It is thought that about forty children attended the school. The building was eventually sold by Reverend James Lawson to

The large building at the front of the view is at the southern end of the village and was divided into two properties in the early twentieth century. One property has always been used to take paying guests. The other side of the property became the Magic Shop. The cottages further along were demolished in 1973, c1905. Author's collection

Robert Dixon who turned it into a private cottage. The money from the sale went towards a new school and the rest was raised by donations. The Earl of Eldon, Ralph Ward Jackson, the Duke of Cleveland and the Shafto family were all contributors. This small school was reported as being 'thinly attended' due to the dependence of the poor on the instruction given at the Sunday Schools.

The National School, belonging to the Church of England, opened on 22 July 1844 on a site in Ashburn Street. The total cost was £630. The first master was Mr Durbin followed by Mr Auty, who was lame and used a crutch. A log of admissions exists with names and ages of the children and names and occupations of the parents. A proper register did not come into being until 1863 when Mr Barker was the master of thirty pupils and Mrs Barker was the mistress. Some of the names that are included in those first registers are from families that still live in Seaton to the present day. Many of those first children were remembered for their achievements in later life. Names such as Lithgo, Lamb, Elstob, Corner, Proctor, Hood, Burton, Watt and Kell are recorded in the very early logs.

The original school was where the church hall now stands. In January 1884, when Mr Dobson was master, a new room was added to the school almost doubling the size of the building. Previously the room had been divided by a curtain to separate the girls from the boys. In 1887 the school came under one head and embraced mixed and infants with Mr Charles Vyvyan Howard as the master. By the twentieth century the school inspectors were complaining about the unsuitability of the school buildings. In 1925 new premises were opened, with facilities for 260 pupils, and the title became Seaton Carew Church of England School.

When Golden Flatts Infant School opened in 1950 and Golden Flatts School in 1951 some of the Seaton pupils were transferred. In July 1953 Seaton became a junior infant school with just one class of senior girls remaining. The school was extended in the 1960s and 70s. In January 2000 the school was renamed Holy Trinity Church of England Primary School. The Bishop of Durham conducted the re-naming ceremony.

Small schools in the area included Mrs Muer's at Grendon House on The Cliff. The following schools were all on the Green. From 1871 to about 1880 there was St Joseph's Academy, a boys' school run by Mr R Johnson. This school had a reputation for efficiency and success. There was great store set on Latin and religious education and French and English recitations. The situation of the school was advertised as being excellent, the front overlooking the Green and the sea, while the back view was of extensive countryside. The academy was in the building that is now 5 the Green. From 1873 to at least 1887 3 and 3A was a seminary for young ladies run by Mrs Maria and Miss Mary Eliza Cowper. From about 1884 to 1886 a school for girls with a kindergarten attached was run by Miss and Mrs Ramsey. The main subjects taught were languages, painting, piano and callisthenics. Mrs Francis Downey also ran a girls' school in 1887. The Misses Haraap and Sterndale ran a girls' school from around 1900 which occupied the two large houses on the west corner of North Road. The school was in existence until at least 1921 but by then it was called Sterndale's School and was run by Alice Sterndale. All these schools were boarding schools. Longhill School was built in 1901 and closed in 1957.

The Seaton Carew Temperance society had 120 juvenile and 60 adult members and the need was felt for a public building for their meetings. The Temperance Hall was erected in Ashburn Street at a cost of £600 donated principally by Edward Backhouse. The building, which could hold 400 people, opened in June 1867. It was said that it was a shame that the prettiest building in the village should be situated in a back street. To make it a day even more memorable for the village the new lifeboat, the *Charlotte*, was presented. In 1900 a Men's Club was erected beside the Temperance Hall. The cost was £700 and the building comprised of a games room with two billiard tables and a reading room. In 1906 there were 80 members.

In 1874 Dr Duncan McCuaig moved from Scotland to Middlesbrough to practise his profession. He was a very talented golf player having won the coveted Gold Medal at the Royal and Ancient Club of St Andrews of which he was a member. When he found there was nowhere to play his beloved game of golf he began looking for somewhere suitable. Lord Eldon owned vast estates in Seaton part of which stretched from the northern end of the village almost to the River Tees. Some of his estate included the Snook at the southern end of the village. Dr McCuaig thought the Snook was an ideal place for his game and rented the land. Lord Eldon was probably only too pleased that a use could be found for the windswept, gorse covered area. Other people interested in golf soon joined the doctor but it was not until 1882 that regular, official appointments were made. At that time the club was named the Durham and Yorkshire Golf Club. Membership crept up slowly and in 1887, with the founding of other clubs, the name was changed to the Seaton Carew Golf Club. In 1891 the golf links opened. As transport became more readily available more and more people joined the club. The club can lay its claim to fame, not only because of the many famous people that have played on its course including the Prince of Wales, but it is the oldest in County Durham and among the first fifty throughout the world.

In August 1874 an auction was held for two properties that are now gone. They were built with the *Seaton Hotel* as attendant lodging houses and were situated on Front Street where the access now is to the hotel car park. The advertisement read:

A dwelling house on the high street and adjoining the Seaton Hotel. It is occupied by Mr TW Wilson and is in use as a beer-house. The house contains, on the ground floor, two rooms and on the second floor, three bedrooms. The yard contains coalhouse, stickhouse and every convenience. There is a good cellar underneath. In the same auction, the dwelling house adjoining the last, and now in the occupation of Miss Barnes as tenant. This house contains the ground floor dining room with spacious room behind fitted with cooking range. On the first floor, large drawing room, four bedrooms and store closet. There is a good cellar kitchen with cooking apparatus and store closet in the basement. In the yard there is every convenience and also a large room with fireplace. The whole property is pleasantly situated commanding a full and uninterrupted view of the sea.

The salt water swimming baths in Seaton were donated by William Gray and opened in 1914. Situated at the north end of the village, the baths were requisitioned by the military during the war. They re-opened to the public in 1951. They closed for the last time in 1976 and were demolished in 1978.

Many of the larger houses became guest houses through the boom years of the late 1960s to 80s. Industry was being built and established and contractors descended on Hartlepool from all corners of the globe. The guest houses, pubs and clubs in Seaton were bursting at the seams. When the work died down there were a few lean years for the businesses until the need for nursing homes became apparent. Some of the large houses were converted to cater for the elderly to fulfil this need. The Gables was one such building. Built in Station Lane in about 1891 by Mr Hogg who was a ship's underwriter, the house was taken over by the RAF from 1916 to 1918 to house the officers from the Seaton Carew airfields. At one time the building served as an unmarried mother's hostel. In 1971 it was bought by the Purvis family and was used as a guesthouse until being converted to Parkview Nursing Home in 1989. A large extension was built to the rear of the property and two sun rooms to the front. Next door to the Gables was Ivycroft which was built and occupied by a doctor. From 1912

The swimming baths situated to the north of the village when they were opened in 1914. The baths were donated by William Gray. A mixture of salt water and chlorine was used. The tram lines, looking like a railway track, can be seen at the front of the building, c1915. Author's Collection

The Waverly Café and Hotel in about 1930. Once known as Yoden House the shop was in use as Crosby's butchers in the latter half of the nineteenth century. Courtesy of Martin Alton

the house belonged to WH Loveridge, an iron merchant. In 1945 planning permission was given for the house to be converted to licensed premises. The house became the Seaton Carew Social Club and Institute.

Hot and cold salt water baths were considered invigorating and a cure for many ailments. There were four lots of baths situated in the village in the nineteenth century. The *Seaton Hotel* had one and from about 1847 James Lithgo was a bath keeper. Between 1851 and 1873 William Proctor advertised his hot and cold baths in Church Street and, as the name implies, Bath House, situated on the corner of Front Street and Crawford Street, was run in the 1850s by Thomas and Elizabeth Crawford. The family were also the proprietors of some of the bathing machines. Sarah Jane, one of their daughters occupied the house until her death in 1915. The other daughter lived in the house until the 1920s. From the late 1920s until the mid 1930s the house was occupied by JF Chapman, an accountant.

The bus station opened in June 1938 to cope with the onslaught of day trippers that came from the colliery villages. It was built by TW Stonehouse, who had also worked on the Staincliffe, in the art deco style. The building made architectural history by being built with the first use of curved concrete. The central clock tower is a single squared shaft on a panelled pedestal.

Longscar Hall was opened in May 1967 to cater for meetings and functions. To most people it has remained a serious blot on the landscape ever since.

Looking towards The Front along Charles Street in 1961. Hartlepool Arts and Museums Collection

Chapter Nine

Village Folk

The wealthy, the poor, the famous and the infamous have moulded Seaton over the years. There are many folk who deserve a mention but the numbers are too numerous. An overall picture of some of the people in the eighteenth and nineteenth centuries will have to suffice.

The early landowners owned large sections of property, which, as they passed away and their heirs took over, would be sold off into smaller and smaller plots. The farms and cottages became affordable to people looking for somewhere to put down roots. The situation must have been ideal compared to the big towns with their cramped houses and smoking chimneys. Seaton was surrounded by fertile farmland, countryside, sea and the River Tees nearby. It is understandable that the Quakers put their

Quaker families on the beach near Staincliffe House in 1881. Although there had been severe storms in August and September of that year the lodging houses in Seaton were still full. The wreck of the French schooner, Alphonse Maria, lies on the beach. On Friday, 26 August, whilst making for Middlesbrough, she struck Longscar and was badly damaged. Captain Calmer and her crew of five saved themselves in an open boat. The rising tide lifted the Alphonse Maria off the rocks and drove her ashore. Courtesy of George Colley

Kitty Bill, the blacksmith, in 1888. Notice his huge arms and blackened face from years of working a forge. Pattison's Pictures

hearts and their wealth into improvements and buildings and established Seaton as a summer resort. Whether in a town or a village life in the Victorian era was hard for the working classes, many toiling long hours just to keep starvation at bay. The visiting Quakers brought work and income to the village. Keeping the visitors carriages in tip-top condition and shoeing their horses would have kept the blacksmith's bellows

Cockle women sitting in front of the rocket house on the slipway from Church Street to the beach, 1888. Pattison's Pictures

working from morning until night. The joiners and builders would be kept in continuous employment erecting new structures and repairing old. With so many feet the village cobblers would hardly have had time to draw breath between making and mending shoes. The butchers and grocers would need to be well stocked in the summer months with the demand for high class fare. The fishing cobles would be out from morning to night, weather permitting, catching the best the North Sea had to offer. In one way or another it can be certain that every Seaton resident benefited from the visiting Quakers.

The beauty and peace of the surroundings attracted merchants and businessmen, such as Thomas Walker and William Thomlinson, to buy existing property or land on which to build their large edifices. Duncan McCuaig wanted somewhere to play

Cockle women posing, none too happily by their serious looks, for their photo in 1888. Pattison's Pictures

Pattison's caption 'Bella's story'. A group of cockle women listen as Bella speaks to them from her beach shack, 1888. Pattison's Pictures

Mrs Elizabeth Hayes Good, landlady of the Seven Stars, at the rear of the inn about to go on a shopping trip, 1889. Pattison's Pictures

Colonel William Thomlinson, Managing Director of Seaton Carew Iron Company. Author's Collection.

golf and Seaton Snooks was the ideal place. He could not have known at the time that his beloved hobby was to found a club that would go down in the annals of history.

For many years an old cannon, without its carriage, had pride of place on the sea-front. The cannon was one of four from the wreck of a man-of-war that foundered at the mouth of the River Tees. One of the cannons was taken to somewhere in the

Pattison's caption 'Howard's children'. The children from the National School in Seaton Carew have a day out with their teacher, Charles V Howard, in 1888. Pattison's Pictures

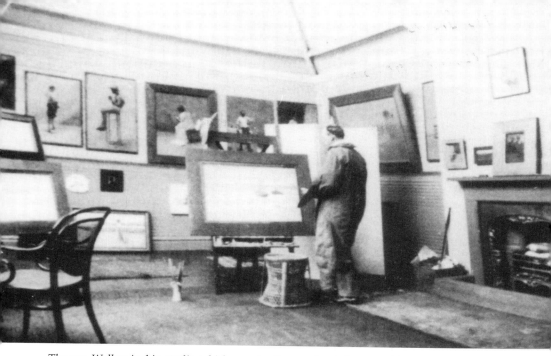

Thomas Walker in his studio which was in the cupola at the top of Staincliffe House.
Courtesy of George Colley

Pattison's caption 'Maude Walker in her studio'. Maude was one of Thomas Walker's daughters, 1888. Pattison's Pictures

Pattison's caption 'The Longscar Belle,' the young lady is one of Thomas Walker's daughters, 1887. Pattison's Pictures

south of England and two were left buried at the site of the wreck. The Seaton cannon was brought to the village by a press-gang and left as a souvenir of their visit. In the 1830s the gun was fired on the occasion of a wedding. Jackie Shute, the bellman, announced that all windows should

Dr Duncan McCuaig, founder of the Durham and Yorkshire Golf Club. The club became Seaton Carew Golf Club in 1887. Author's Collection

be left open or they would run the risk of being broken, as indeed some of them were. Old Peggy Appleby, who wore a man's coat and smoked a cutty pipe, lit the fuse. Peggy had been at sea for many years as a man before the mast. After this event the cannon was embedded in the sea wall near Franklin's Corner with its muzzle protruding, where it remained until 1878. The villagers then moved it to the grass on the sea-front. In 1887, on Queen Victoria's Golden Jubilee, the cannon was fired once more. This time the fuse was lit by James Lithgo. He had no experience in these matters and the backfire from the powder marked him for life. During the war all metal, including old guns, were collected for scrap. A council worker had the forethought to put the Seaton cannon to one side and when the war ended it was given to the Hartlepool Yacht Club. It was used by the club as a starting gun and was fired by Jim Atkinson senior, ex Royal Artillery. When it had served its active life it was removed and placed in a private garden.

In the nineteenth century an old man called Jackie Franklin would buy pebbles collected from the beach by the children. He then polished the pebbles and sold them to visitors as souvenirs.

In February 1866 a man appeared, seemingly from nowhere, and made his abode about half-way down Seaton Snook. He had a wild appearance with old-fashioned shabby clothes and a long unkempt beard. He introduced himself as Timon and thereafter became known as Timon of the Tees. His 'house' was the body of an old carriage which was secured to the bottom of a kind of yacht, not much bigger than a fisherman's coble. In this tiny dwelling he had a small table, seats, shelves and a fireplace. Timon's boat cost 10s (50p), his buggy, which he used to collect things from the beach, cost 7s 6d (38p) and the freehold to live on the Snook cost

Pattison's caption '85 years old in October 1889,' a portrait of Mrs Burton. Pattison's Pictures

17s 6d (88p). He had obtained a bad habit since his arrival in Seaton, he had learned to smoke. Although considered a strange character, Timon was inoffensive and harmless. His mind seemed to wander and he often talked rubbish but it was thought that he had been well educated as he

Captain Bunting, Miss Stavely and her brother, William Richard Stavely, Custom House Officer, relaxing on the rocks in 1889. Pattison's Pictures

read from old law books. Timon attended Holy Trinity Church twice every Sunday. He lived mainly on fish and shellfish and was grateful for any offerings of food that the good people of Seaton offered. In June of 1866 he left his house one day to see what pickings there were on the beach. When he returned it was to find that he had been burgled and some of his possessions, including books and documents, had been burned. The general feeling was that the offence had been committed by cockle women

A group posing on the beach in front of the lowlight in 1889. Miss Stavely is seated on the right and her brother, Willy, is standing. Willy's dress sense is rather incongruous; he is wearing a jacket and cravat with waders. Pattison's Pictures

from West Hartlepool. Timon said that amongst the missing articles were a coat and a pair of 'unmentionables' but these were later returned to him.

Timon told a reporter for the *South Durham Herald* that he was a landed proprietor, owning the Cleveland Hills and the Kirkleatham Estates. The documents that had been burnt were the evidence that he had collected over the years to prove his rights. Timon insisted that far from being a mindless act of vandalism, it was one of his half siblings who had destroyed this evidence intentionally. His words to the reporter were: '*Mind Sir, there's eleven of the same name as nursed me; and he didn't admit it until he was on his death bed*'. It is highly unlikely that Timon had a claim on any property; these would just have been the ramblings of an old man. Some good came of his misfortune as, after the occurrence, the villagers visited the hermit on a regular basis. Timon remained at Seaton until 1873.

William Thomlinson was born in Houghton-le-Spring in 1854. From 1870 he worked in the iron industry in Tennessee until his return to Britain in 1882 when he bought 10 the Green. He was a member of the first West Hartlepool Town Council, a Justice of the Peace and served in the local volunteer regiment rising to the rank of Lieutenant Colonel. Thomlinson was appointed Deputy Lieutenant of County Durham and in 1936 received a knighthood. He married the daughter of Thomas Kirk who was Managing Director of the Seaton Carew Iron Company. When Kirk died in 1906 Thomlinson took his place. The Seaton Iron Company was bought

Mary Ferguson at the age of seventy with a sea-coal rake and basket; she died the year after this photo was taken, in 1888. Pattison's Pictures

over by Dorman Long in 1920 and this made Thomlinson a very wealthy man. By his retirement in 1924 he owned a large proportion of land within Seaton. He died in 1943 at the age of 89. Thomlinson was described as a rather alarming man who could be friendly at times. Locals remember that when they were children, if they played too near his house, he would bang on the window with his stick. Through his life Thomlinson spent a lot of time travelling to the east and the orient. He amassed a fabulous collection

Pattison's caption, 'The village fathers', Henry Storer, George Burlinson, Robert Corner and Arthur Robson, the postman. The little boy looks a proper toff in his cap and breeches, 1888. Pattison's Pictures

of Chinese eighteenth century porcelain, oriental Buddha's and Hindu deities, some of which he donated to the Gray Art Gallery and Museum in 1922 and the rest after his death.

Some of the children that first attended the National School also achieved some measure of fame in later life. Henry Lamb was admitted to the school in 1854 at the age of three. A log in the school

Pattison's caption, 'Laying down the law': Ralph Noddings on the left and George Burlinson on the right outside the general dealers on Front Street, probably Bowser and Sons. The sign states 'Tea Dealers. Ale, Porter and Tobacco,' 1888. Pattison's Pictures

George Burlinson, Bowser Simms and Robert Hovel with a bucket and mop. The Tees must have needed a valet, 1888. Pattison's Pictures

record dated 20 July 1863 states: *'Examined standard IV, in dictation, results very low: Henry Lamb 12 mistakes in 22 lines; H Lamb in arithmetic, only 1 wrong'.* An entry a year or so later states: *'Henry Lamb and William Hood (Standard V) being the only boys right. November, Henry Lamb the only boy right in dictation'.* Henry Lamb went on to become a Town Councillor for West Hartlepool. How the pupils received any kind of education must surely have been down to excellent

Pattison's caption 'Kay, a Seaton professional' playing in front of the Seaton Carew Golf Club House in 1888. Andrew Kay was a legend at the game of golf in his time. Pattison's Pictures

Ness and the young Burton listening to Bob Johnson playing his whistle, 1888. Pattison's Pictures

teaching by the various masters and mistresses because they seemed to spend more time out of the classroom than in. Sometimes they would have to stay at home to help with chores but any excuse to miss lessons was used. Harvesting, a wedding, a shipwreck, lifeboat practice, everything and anything would entice the pupils away from their desks.

Chapter Ten

Tragedies & Incidents

In April 1543 Henry Lackenby of Seaton Carew stood trial before Dr Clyff at York on suspicion of heresy in the reign of Henry VIII, the result of his trial is not recorded but he would probably have faced execution. In 1569, during the rebellion of the Nothern Earls, the rebels stole *'a sylver pece'* from James Lackenby, the vicar of Stranton. In the same year a member of the parish was executed as a rebel. The silver piece must have been recovered because it was left in the vicar's will as *'the pece that was stolen'* to his sister's son. In 1673 John Harrison, a cripple, killed Thomas Smailes, a glazier, with his crutch. Harrison was hanged. A plague began on 21 May 1597 and lasted throughout the summer. In 1849 a cholera epidemic claimed many lives within the area.

An entry that was supposed to have been taken from a book, written by HV Illingsworth, tells us that the Green, between 1635 and 1721, was used as a hanging green. Unfortunately all my efforts and those of the Hartlepool Reference Library and British Library to track down the authenticity of the book, the author and the existence of the people mentioned in the document have been to no avail. It was quite common in the eighteenth and nineteenth centuries for fictional tales to be written about a place that was real and for the story to be published in broadsheets. Because there were stocks on the Green until 1870, I felt it was possible there might have also been a gibbet erected there at some time. Unless further information surfaces at some time in the future it must be assumed that the following is fiction but I still thought it worthy of inclusion.

The first to be hanged on the green is said to be one, Lisa Row, a fair maid of seventeen summers who didst receive into her possession 1 loaf of oatmeal bread and 2 quarts of milk, the property of Thomas Bowes, Master Baker of Prospect Place, Seaton Carew in the County of Durham. Sentence of death was placed upon the child by the visiting Magistrate, Nicholas Wreston and during the noon the sentence was carried out on a gloomy November day, 1635. The same Magistrate that day sentenced Robert Cragg Fowlster of Crescent Cottage to 100 lashes of the tail for uttering a foul oath during the Sabbath. It is recorded that Robert Cragg died the next day. During the Magistrates sitting the following items were devoured by the peace men, three gallons of ale, four pounds of cheese and four butter loaves. The total cost was five shillings and one and a half pennies. In the week recorded, the Magistrate retired to his seat at Durham and there sentenced five men, three children and six women to death. He died in 1643 at the age of sixty-five. On his tombstone; a noble and just man at peace.

On Saturday, 1 December 1866, the Betsy Williams, carrying a cargo of timber, ran aground at the Teesmouth. The vessel belonged to Wade and Sons who contacted their underwriters to clarify their position in regard to insurance. They were told that they must make every effort possible to salvage the cargo. The manager, Mr Mitchell, sent twenty men, most of them Irish, furnished with implements to pull the cargo into shore as it floated from the vessel. Six of the tools the men were furnished with for the job were pikes. The weather was freezing and, after about five hours work, the men were cold, tired and hungry. Most of the group headed for the *Seven Stars* but Anthony Leonard and another man went to the *Seaton Hotel*, leaving the pikes in the lobby as they entered.

They ordered their drinks and food and began chatting to the servant, Emma Gray, who asked them what the pikes were for. The men told her they were Fenians and the pikes were weapons with which they were going to take over the village. Poor Emma was terrified and ran to tell the landlady, Mrs Sothren. She, in turn, took fright and asked a man, Dobing, to stand in as deputy landlord while she went for the police and sent word of the threat around the village. Thomas Baines was the local constable and he hurried to the hotel. As he passed up Front Street he noticed a lot of strangers hanging about. On entering the hotel the PC spoke to Dobing. As they were talking a man came into the room carrying a pike. The man, who was Leonard, pointed the pike towards the deputy landlord and threatened to run him through. The PC told Leonard to put the pike down but his companion appeared also brandishing a pike and threatening the constable. Baines and Dobing eventually managed to disarm the two men and eject them from the hotel. Because there were so many Irishmen about the village, the PC decided it would be prudent not to make an arrest at that time. At the *Seven Stars* the villagers, believing the stories about the Fenian invasion, had ejected all the strangers from the inn. The men were standing outside when their boss, Mr Mitchell, arrived and asked why they were not at the Snook pulling in the cargo. The men all skedaddled back to West Hartlepool. By this time the West Hartlepool police were preparing to head for Seaton to '*quell the riot*'.

John Mitchell, Manager of Wade and Sons. Mitchell sent about twenty men to the Snook to salvage the timber from the Betsy. The men later caused the 'Fenian Invasion' of Seaton. Author's Collection

Seven Stars Hotel from where the 'Fenians' were evicted by the locals in 1866. John Mitchell saw the men loitering outside and with a word from him they scurried back to West Hartlepool, 1853. Photo by Edward Backhouse, Pattison's Pictures

On Monday morning the Newcastle papers stated that Seaton Carew had been attacked by at least fifty armed Fenians in a scene of bloodshed and riot. The locals, aided by the police, had exhibited their loyalty by putting down the miscreants. As the week went on this much embellished story was in all the major newspapers, even as far as London.

Leonard appeared in court charged with being drunk and assaulting PC Baines. It was decided that it had been a joke that had backfired and he had been a little the worse for drink. Also, that the whole story had been so exaggerated by the tabloids that the case could not be judged properly. Leonard was released without penalty.

Sadly, accidents were all too common in industry in the nineteenth century. Two accidents occurred in 1887 resulting in loss of life. In July there was an explosion at the Cliff House Ironworks. A boiler, that had been inspected just beforehand and declared safe, burst. The force was so strong it lifted from its seat and travelled about eighty feet. Two young boys and six men were caught in the blast. Benjamin Doherty, a young boy, was killed immediately and Thomas Sutherland, who was fourteen, died at his home the following day. Two of the men died later and the other four were expected never to be able to work again.

On 12 October of the same year a group of men who had been out of work for some time were given employment by a contractor, Mr Coultas, at Seaton Ironworks Blast Furnaces. Their job was to dig out a blast furnace so it could be re-lined. They were digging a hole through the old brickwork when suddenly a rush of cinders and flame came from the hole enveloping everyone in its path. Their workmates nearby were quick to go to the rescue but seven of the men were burnt, four of them seriously. They were all put in cabs to be taken home where they would be treated by Dr Samuel Biggart. One man died almost immediately and another two, who had been almost skinned, were then moved to hospital but both died the following day. The three fatalities were James McNally, William Reed and William Glear.

Being on the coast, the inns and hotels of Seaton were the last resting places before the grave of many a drowned sailor and deaths in other circumstances. There are many records of post-mortems and inquests being held in public buildings. A jar or two of ale would perhaps take the edge off this unpleasant task. In the *Seaton Hotel* there was a room set aside for the purpose of laying out dead bodies. One evening in February 1901 an Irishman, John Foeney, who had lived in the locality for about twenty years, was in the hotel and left very drunk. Foeney worked for Mr Elstob at Hunter House Farm and must have made his way back there. He slept in an outbuilding that had a calf-house below and a granary above. Later that night an alarm was given that the outbuilding was on fire. The fire brigade, which was stationed three miles away, took twenty-eight minutes to arrive. When the fire was eventually brought under control, Foeney's body was found hanging suspended from the joists of the granary. It was thought, that in his drunken state, he had either knocked a candle over or

Cliff House Iron Works where four men died due to an explosion in 1887. Courtesy of George Colley

dropped his pipe and started the fire. It was ironic that his body should be taken to the very place for a post-mortem where he had bought the drink that ultimately caused his death.

In September 1916 a brawl broke out at the *Seaton Hotel*. It was between a group of about twenty-five Belgians who worked at the Zinc Works and some local men. It is difficult to determine who started the argument, each group blaming the other. It appears that it was racially motivated. When the local policeman was called he could not quell the brawl on his own so called for help. A sergeant and four members of the police force and four military personnel arrived to give assistance. In the course of the events that followed one of the Belgians, Karel Verees, was stabbed with a bayonet. He later died from his injuries. At the inquest into the death it was stated that Verees had a knife. No weapon was found on his person at the time but one of his co-workers did have a knife. It was never discovered who struck the fatal blow but the verdict that was given, after rather patchy evidence, was one of justifiable homicide.

In April 1949 a terrible fire broke out in the prop fields. The timber used for pit props was stored in an area of sixty-five acres at Carr House. Each stack of timber held about 200 logs. The fire started in an area behind the *Staincliffe Hotel*. At the time the wind was blowing from the south-west. Had it changed direction or become any stronger the consequences could have been disastrous. Flames up to fifty feet high could be seen from all over Teesside. Men, women and children volunteered their help to try and put out the fire. Men helped with the blaze, women made tea and

The pit prop fire that caused devastation in 1949. Courtesy of George Colley

sandwiches for the exhausted fire-fighters and the children helped to pull the fire-hoses along. The water pressure was limited from the fire-hoses because of the distance along Coronation Drive the hoses had to stretch. Water was used from the nearby beck but it was found to contain creosote which would only fuel the fire. It was decided to use suction pumps to draw sea-water, even though the salt and sand would damage the equipment, it was decided that was an acceptable risk. Later it was found that the pumps were in need of repair due to the damage caused. Homes around Lawson Road had been evacuated, furniture was carted away to be stored in the Temperance Hall, the school and other large buildings. Huts and other structures on the allotments were destroyed and huge stacks of timber moved so that the fire had nothing to feed on. Eventually all civilians were told to leave while twenty or so fire brigades and about 1000 troops battled for thirty six hours until the fire was eventually brought under control. A rough estimate of the damage was £500,000 but no lives were lost. A few men were treated for burns and one man was hit in the mouth by a swinging prop. He stopped long enough to spit out a couple of loose teeth and then carried on with what he was doing. A couple visiting from California had been staying in one of the houses that were at risk. The gentleman was later heard to comment 'All this is a great pity, but I must say it seems the only way to warm the place up'.

Chapter Eleven

Shore & Sea

11.1 Flotsam & Jetsam

In *Fell's Guide to Sunken Treasure* it is recorded that on 4 June 1669 a vessel, believed to be a Spanish galleon, sank in Seaton Bay. The vessel was named the *Little Duck* and had sailed from the Netherlands carrying £300,000 worth of gold and silver specie. Two hundred years later the villagers were given the opportunity to live in luxury for a time. On a Saturday night in March 1867 a severe storm with high winds blew the sand from the beach revealing the clay and peat beneath. The following day dawned fine and clear. Two men were walking across the sands on their way to Middlesbrough to seek work. The tide was out, and as they were passing close to the Longscar rocks, one of them dropped his pipe. As he bent to pick it up he spied something curious in amongst the seaweed. On picking the object up and cleaning the black muck from it he realised it was a silver coin. A quick search of the immediate area revealed hundreds more coins, both of silver and gold. The two men picked up what they could carry and, returning to the village, sold the lot. They then headed straight into the public house for a good drinking session. The news of the find spread around Seaton like wildfire. The rest of that day and all through the night the beach was lit up by the lanterns of crowds of people riddling the sand to try and find every last coin. The Lord of the Manor tried to claim the treasure, but he was too late, the villagers, with lightning speed, had changed everything they had picked up into currency they could spend. The following letter was sent to a local newspaper shortly after the treasure had been found:

By a Retired Jordie (Geordie) *Keelman*
Tawkin' fornet lock-oots, what de ye think o' the Hartleypeul torn-ups mistor? A varry dollor-is iccount hes bin fordid to me biv a Hartleypeul toon Coonsillor an two iv his chums, that's Mr Richard Varlow, Captin McCarthy an Benjymin Roome, the Sporrit Rapper o' Hartleypeul, consarnin' the goold an' silvor mine thit's bin fund on the beach thair sor. Two half-rockt layborrers gan dandorrin' illang be the see-side the tuther day, happind te drop on tiv a-peety reef o' rocks an the doddil o' won o' the cheps pipes teuk intiv it's heed te fawl on te this see-weed gardin. Tommy stoopt down te pick the doddil up when he seed what te him leakt like a black penny lyin' close te the reekin baccy. Tommy picks hor up, rubs hor a bit, finds oot she's silvor, an cawls on his meyt thit wos wawkin on iffore him, te cum back. Annuther an annuther, an still lots iv uthers torns up thor black bellies fra the peet. What's te be deun noo Tommy? Says red-haired Dick

Man. Thore croon pecies, but thor nut iv onny king's rain thit aw naw on. Heer's Carrillis,, but who Carrillis wis aw naw nowt, xsept it wis Juwlyis Seesor. Se te the Joo they gans an sells thor prizis for two or three bob a peece, an awa they gans an gets bleezin drunk, blow the gaff, an lets the cat oot o' the poke. Next day thor's hundords o' foaks seekin the dollor-is trisshor an putten black munny in thor pockits. Fond feuls, them layborrers mit hae gathort a little fortin had they oney kep the luck spot te thorsils, but like the cats, they cuddent fare weel an had thor gobs. It's thowt thit a ship hid geyn doon heer loded wi' silvor an goold munny, is the price o' a cargo o' slaves, an the silvor coins, nawin the unholy porchise o' yewmin flesh, hid torned black in the feyce, an cum to the sorfis o' the see, like pigs in Paddy's land wif a nife an fork in thor gobs, skweekin' oot, who'll find me? Aw hope maw Harleypeul cronies Varlow, Roome an Cumpny dissent gan upon the battor it law tide howkin oot the black feyced charleys, sor. No, no they waddent file thor fingers wi' the blud munny o' the poor slaves. Se aw heer thim say, sor.

The other story relating to this incident was that a collier, sailing from London, was wrecked at Seaton in 1829. She was carrying about £300 worth of silver dollars, gold coins and rings. When the vessel was dismantled at the time some coins were said to have been found. The sand then covered the remains of the wreck until the storm revealed the site again in 1867. The vessel was said to be a Spanish slaver and the treasure, which was hidden in her timbers, being payment for human cargo. The English were supposed to have captured the ship and re-named her the *Duck*. There is mention of some of the silver dollars that were found on the beach in 1867 being from the reign of Carolus the III and IV dated 1740 to 1804. If this is correct then the treasure could not have come from the galleon of earlier date. There is in existence, however, an earlier coin from the reign of Carolus II so perhaps it was these that were found. Certainly the treasure must have come from a wrecked vessel but from which is impossible to prove as no-one at the time was saying anything and now there is no-one left to tell the tale. Lying on the seabed or under the sand time and tide would rot the wood and leave non perishable cargo behind with few clues as to how it came to be there.

The mighty North Sea and its coastline are the holders of many untold secrets. However, down through the ages, scribes and historians have recorded some of the events and tragedies that have taken place on the shores of Seaton Carew.

Although there was a Lord of the Manor, it was the Bishop of Durham that had 'Right of Wreck,' which meant anything considered of value to wash up onto the beach belonged to him. This might include a ship and its cargo or a large fish. Although the royal fish was depicted as a sturgeon it is more likely the fish that were on this coastline would have been whales. In Hutchinson's *History of Durham*:

On 21st November 1766 a spermaceti whale, seventeen yards long, (almost 7m) was caught at the mouth of the Tees by a ship coming from Newcastle to Stockton. It was towed into Seaton and was dead when it touched the ground. It made such a noise that it could be heard several miles off.

There are numerous records of the Right of Wreck being infringed. In the early thirteenth century Peter de Brus, Lord of Skelton, disputed the Bishop's Right of Wreck and he and his servants carried away a boat that was washed up at Seaton. Gerard de Seton reported him to the Bishop. De Brus was fined 50s (£2.50) and in revenge he had de Seton arrested and clapped in a dungeon at Skelton Castle. The Bishop retaliated by excommunicating all those involved in the arrest and setting Seton free. De Brus was fined an extra £20 and was so angry at what he considered unjust treatment, two great barons were sent for to settle the quarrel. It resulted in de Brus being excused his fines providing he agreed the Bishop would have his Right of Wreck in the future. As a perpetual memorial of this agreement the mainmast of the next wreck was to be fashioned into a cross and erected on a hill called Blake Law by the side of the road from Hartlepool to Sadberge so that any traveller might see it. From the same vessel a candlestick was made and placed in Sadberge Church.

In 1342 John de Carrow appears in a record in the Court of Bishop Bury. He had seized a whale that had been cast upon the shore and divided the fish amongst his friends. He acknowledged the trespass and was fined 100 marks. In about 1457 Thomas and Margaret Lumley had a Grant of Wrecks within their manor between Stranton and Seaton. In 1621 Robert Johnson, a yeoman of Greatham, seized a fish that was cast upon the shore at Seaton. At the bishop's court it was decided that the fish was a royal fish and therefore belonged to the bishop:

Robert Preston, John Wilton, John Dent, Robert Harrison in right of Anne, his wife, Rev J Horseman, Rev T Drake, Cuthbert Scurfield, and Nicholas and Robert Chilton, both of Carr House floated a part wreck taken by those who they claim in 1709 and 1727, a mast that had been cast up near Carr House in 1729, in 1730, a quantity of bale goods, in 1736 the keel of a ship cast up near Seaton Snook, and in 1754 a mast. At the hearing on April 11th, 1770 the case was dismissed without costs.

In 1235 the villagers buried the bodies of four sailors that were washed ashore but because they had not informed the coroner, they were fined at Sadberge. In December 1785 in a violent storm, not less than 33 vessels were stranded on the beach between Hartlepool and Seaton. On 17 February 1836 at Seaton the water flowed through the street like a river, a vessel went on shore and all hands perished. On 16 February 1838 a violent storm brought water pouring through the streets of Seaton. A vessel was washed ashore, nineteen houses in New Stranton were flooded and a newly built public house at Haverton Hill was completely demolished. In June 1855 the body of an infant was found floating near to Carr House. At the inquest at the *King's Head Inn* it was concluded that the baby had been murdered by being allowed to bleed to death before being dumped in the water. The perpetrator was never discovered. On 29 June 1856 three young men, Brown and Pearson who were apprenticed to Watson & Co drapers, and Harrison, apprenticed to Mill & Co grocers, went swimming in Seaton Bay. A wreck had recently been removed and the young men fell into the hole that was left and drowned. On 28 May 1860 a severe storm caused many vessels to be stranded at Redcar, Hartlepool and Seaton. Sheep and cattle in great numbers were found dead. In January 1887 the body of a man was washed up on the beach and taken to the *Seaton Hotel* for a post mortem and inquest. His face was so badly bruised he was not identifiable and the verdict of the jury was 'found dead'. In May 1886 a sailor was washed up on the shore and buried by the villagers. He was thought to be a crew-member from the *Isis* that had been wrecked a few days previously.

11.2 Wrecks & Rescues
Before the breakwaters were erected the coastline around Seaton was hazardous. The sands faced north-east to the North Sea and were between the cliffs of Cleveland and the cliffs of Durham. At a place between the Green and the Staincliffe, just a little way out to sea, there was a spot marked on the charts as the Wreck Hole. A little way from shore was Littlescar and Longscar, dangerous shelves of rocks that would be hidden when the tide was high. The wind would roar in towards the unprotected bay sweeping everything in its path before it. The wooden sailing vessels with their flimsy sails did not stand a chance and it is known there have been thousands wrecked and countless lives lost between Redcar and Hartlepool. Two lighthouses were erected in 1838. The highlight at Longhill, situated near what is now Windermere Road, was a Tuscan column of magnesium limestone with an internal spiral staircase lit by slit windows. The tower supported a lantern. The whole structure was moved in the twentieth century to the Marina as a memorial to the town's shipping roots and as a tourist attraction. The lowlight was situated to the north of the Staincliffe on The Cliff where Queen Street now ends. The double lights, one shining above the other, were to warn seafarers from a long way out to sea of the hazards they were approaching. Sometimes, as well as storms, darkness and the tremendous force of the sea, there would also be thick fog that would roll over everything like a blanket. The lighthouse lanterns would then be useless. In 1869 a lighthouse inspection was carried out by a Trinity House inspector. The ensuing report declared the gas lamps and apparatus unsuitable, dirty and imperfect and recommended a complete reorganisation. Another warning was the bell-buoy on the Longscar. An early map marks the Longscar as Blackstones, presumably because of their extremely dark colour. The danger of the rocks was pointed out in a heartrending poem written by a lady visiting in the summer of 1864:

Oh come not near me, 'tis dangerous ground,
The bones of mariners lie scattered around,
I mark the spot where the brave ones fell,
Come not near me I am the Longscar Bell.
As wave follows wave I rise and fall,
The higher the roll, the louder I call,
The first ones to hear me be the first ones to tell
When coming towards me, the Longscar Bell.
I'll cease not to sound forth my sad, sad lay
You can hear me at night,
You may see me by day,
Whoever pass by me mark me well,
For danger lies hid near the Longscar Bell.
Then come not near me, come not near,
The young and the old are buried here,
I mark the spot where the brave ones fell
Come not near me, I am the Longscar Bell.

In February 1865 there were two local incidents where, it appears, that money was more important than human life. The first incident was when a gale had been blowing for a full day and the screw steamer *Mulgrave* was laying at anchor. A steam tug tried to tow her in but the rope broke. The winds were so strong that the vessel was being dragged towards the Longscar Rocks with her anchor down. Six men manned a tugboat and, after a struggle, managed to attach a rope to her. They then made a bargain with the

Seaton lowlight situated on The Cliff at the end of Queen Street on the seaward side of the road at a spot locally known as Lighthouse Corner. Hartlepool Arts and Museums Collection

At a meeting held in April of 1900, regarding the renewal and widening of the road at the northern end of the village, a question was asked as to what would become of Lighthouse Corner. The reply was that all was in hand; it certainly was, the lighthouse was doomed. This image is during the demolition of the lowlight. Author's Collection

captain that for £150 they would tow her into port. The deal was made and the vessel was towed to safety. Apparently bargains such as this were quite common. The second incident should have had the villagers hanging their heads in shame. The *Thomas and Margaret*, a fishing lugger from Whitby with a crew of nine, attempted to get into the West Harbour. She was caught by heavy seas which took away her mainsail. The craft began to drift towards Seaton but before she reached shore she ran aground. The sea was washing over the lugger but eventually the crew managed to launch a small boat and climb in. Almost immediately the tiny boat was swamped and the nine men were drowned. After a while the lugger washed ashore with its cargo of fish. A crowd had gathered on the beach and three fellows waded into the water to grab the compass box. Someone on the beach took it from them and ran away. The mob gave chase and a fight broke out over the possession of the box. The brother of the captain of the lugger was there and said the box should be his. The crowd began to get rough with him and if it had not been for the arrival of the coastguard he would have been in dire straits. Even when the coastguard took possession of the box the crowd threatened to stone him.

Another find on Seaton beach, this time spelling catastrophe, was in September 1933. The wreckage of a plane, including two wheels, an axle and a shock absorber were discovered. They had come from an RAF plane of No. 40 Bomber Squadron of Abingdon. The plane had been heard to crash into the waters of Hartlepool Bay in thick fog on 26 September. Although the Hartlepool lifeboat and many other small fishing craft conducted a search the bomber's two airmen were lost.

Other heartbreaking stories include observers seeing masts falling into the sea with men still clinging to the rigging, the lifeboat being near enough for the crew to grasp someone's hand only for a wave to snatch them away, one of the crew of the lifeboat had hold of the jacket sleeve of

A sketch of the Charlotte going to the aid of the Jesse Stevens in 1849. Pattison's Pictures

a sailor from the *Marquis of Huntley* only for the sleeve to tear and come away in the would be rescuer's hand.

On 2 August 1833 the brig *Cephalus* of Middlesbrough, carrying a cargo of coal, when leaving the *Tees* towed by a steam tug became stranded on the South Knoll off Seaton. When signals of distress were seen the Seaton lifeboat, *Tees*, was launched. They took off six men and a boy before the *Cephalus* became a total wreck. Thomas Thompson, the Master, and William Francis, the mate, were both drunk. The rest of the crew consisted of George Ridley, William Shotton, James Gray and his son, who was just a young boy, and one other sailor. The crew of the lifeboat were William Hood, Arthur and William Brown, James Lithgo, Robert Hunter, Thomas Wilson, John Henry, John Proctor, Richard Hayes, Christopher Bell, William Hartburn, William Walker and Thomas White. There were also helpers to get the horses ready to pull the boat and get it into the water. Robert Shildon, a pilot of Redcar, who assisted in the rescue, suffered a dislocated hip. On this particular rescue the costs were as follows; the salary for the coxswain was £1.1s (£1 5p) each member of the crew was paid 10s 6d (52p), the helpers, of which there would be at least ten, were paid between 6d and 1s each (2p-5p) and for the use of each horse, of which there were eight, 5s (25p). The crew would then go to one of the public houses in the village to quench their thirst and heat their bodies. A bill from the *Seaton Hotel* in 1837 when the lifeboat had taken off the crew of the distressed *Evenwood* came to 15s (75p) for ale and rum, which would be paid for from the lifeboat's funds.

A sketch of the John Lawson going to the aid of the Granite, depicted in the Illustrated London News in 1888. Author's Collection

Friday, 8 February 1861 one of the worst ever storms in the area was recorded. Although hundreds of lives were saved by the six local lifeboats that worked none stop for the duration of the storm, more than 60 were lost. It was estimated that around seventy vessels were wrecked, many on the Longscar. From these treacherous rocks the Seaton lifeboat crew managed to save eight men from the *Providence,* eight from the *Mayflower* and five from a crew of eleven from the *Robert Watson,* the other six saving themselves in their own boat. An unknown brig and schooner, the *Alliance* with six men and the *Warnsbeck* with eight men were wrecked with loss of all hands as the crew of the lifeboat and people on shore watched helplessly. The Seaton boat went out six times on that one day. It was said later that after the storm you could reach the town pier at Hartlepool from Seaton by clambering over the beached wrecks without your feet touching the sand. In the log of the Return of Wreck after that terrible storm Robert Hood, coxswain of the *Charlotte,* wrote:

Saturday, 9th February 1861. Yesterday a brig was seen drifting towards the Longscar Rocks. The Seaton Carew and the Hartlepool lifeboats were launched at the same moment. They used every endeavour to reach the crew but to no avail. In the meantime another schooner also stuck on the rocks at the same place. Both ships became total wrecks with the loss of all hands.

The names of both vessels and the number of lives lost remain unknown. Wherever they came from their families would wait in vain for their return never knowing what had become of their fathers, brothers, uncles, husbands and sons.

On 8 December 1866 a Newcastle steamer, the *Wrecker,* with the Captain and two crew members, got into difficulties near the South Gare. At this time the Seaton lifeboat could not be launched because the coxswain, Henry Hood, had gone to Newcastle for the day and had left no instructions with anyone for dealing with an emergency should it arise. A Middlesbrough steam-tug, the *Swan,* went to the vessel's assistance but could not get near enough to perform a rescue. George Cowell, a local man, was aboard the *Swan* and, seeing the predicament of the men on the *Wrecker,* he launched a small boat to try and get close enough to get the crew off. Within minutes of leaving the tug his boat was swamped and he was drowned. Meanwhile the Captain of the *Wrecker* launched the steamer's little boat and rowed himself to safety leaving the other two men to their fate. A boat belonging to Trinity House was launched from the Snook and the two remaining crew were saved. The Captain said that he had not deserted his crew but had been trying to save George Cowell. He was not believed. Because Cowell had given his life to try and save others his widow was taken care of from the RNLI funds.

On 24 December 1869, during a gale, the schooner *Mary Young* ran into difficulties. The crew were saved by the Seaton lifeboat but the vessel with her cargo of timber was wrecked. On the same night the *Daisy,* carrying a cargo of sleepers, was in trouble but by the time the lifeboat reached her all the crew had either jumped or been washed overboard. The barque *Antagonist* was towed into harbour badly damaged.

In October 1870 the *Souter Johnny,* carrying over 100 tons of grain, foundered between the pier and the Longscar Buoy. Two men and a woman were rescued by the tug *William* but the vessel and her cargo was lost. In January 1871 eight colliers were approaching Hartlepool when they lost their way in the fog and became stuck on Longscar Rocks. Luckily it stayed calm and they were able to float off on the morning tide. In May 1871 five men, four of them between eighteen and twenty and one only fifteen, went out to sea in a light, four oar racing gig. There had been warnings of sudden squalls which they ignored. They were spotted after an hour or so just rowing round the harbour. Later, when they did not return, the steam tug *Charlie* went to search for them. It met with two pilots in their cobles towing the ill-fated skiff between them. All five young men had drowned. In 1875 Henry Hood, coxswain of the *Job Hindley* wrote:

21st October 1875 at about 6pm signals of distress were observed from a vessel on the North Gare. The lifeboat was launched but after two hours no lights could be seen on the dark and very stormy sea so the boat proceeded to the shore. On 22nd October at about 2.30am a portion of the vessel with two masts still standing was observed. The lifeboat was again launched and took eight men in an exhausted state from the mizzen rigging.

The three-masted schooner, *Auld Reekie* of Middlesbrough carrying a cargo of pitch, was totally wrecked but all the crew were saved.

Many other tragedies were recorded but perhaps none in such detail as the one that took place on 12 November 1888. The *Granite* was a brig from West Hartlepool owned by Mr Jefferson of Scarborough Street. The brig had sailed from London with a crew of seven under Captain Leug and a cargo of loam and was in sight of home when disaster struck. She was making her way towards the Teesmouth when the coastguard on duty realised she was in difficulty. The new lifeboat, the *John Lawson*, was launched on her first rescue mission. The conditions were so bad that it took an hour to get within reach of the *Granite*. News had reached Middlesbrough of the vessel's plight and five powerful tugs were sent to assist. The crowd that was congregated on the shore at the Snook watched in horror as the drama unfolded. They could see the crew clinging for dear life to the rigging. The rescue boats tried again and again to get near enough to the stricken brig for the crew to jump to safety. The seas were too high and too strong and every attempt failed. The Middlesbrough lifeboat arrived to assist but to no avail. Nearly four hours after the rescue had been launched, the mast of the brig fell carrying most of the crew with it. Those that were left clung to the forecastle. One poor wretch jumped and swam towards the rescue boats but he sank from sight before reaching safety. By now those that were left alive were clinging on to bits of

A map showing the position of the many wrecks on the North East coast, from the Wreck Chart of the British Isles for 1855. Compiled by the Board of Trade. Hartlepool Arts and Museums Collection

wreckage. One by one the cold and exhaustion became too much for them and they disappeared beneath the waves.

Amongst the watching crowd was sixty-eight year old Miss Strover, a well respected member of the Seaton community. The trauma of the day proved too much for her and she collapsed and died of a heart attack.

On 1 October 1912 the Swedish schooner *Presto* struck rocks at North Gare. The lifeboat could not get near to the vessel because of the violent seas and the rocks. Harry Cross, coastguard, procured a stout rope and managed to lasso the mast of the stricken vessel. All the crew and helpers pulled on the rope until the mast bent and the men aboard were able to crawl along the timber to safety. The captain was the last to leave but as he made his way along the mast it snapped and he fell to his death on the rocks below. He was the last person to lose his life during a rescue attempt by the Seaton boat.

The last sailing ship to be wrecked at Seaton was the *Doris* on 26 September 1930. Her crew of nine were saved by the first motorised boat from Hartlepool, the *Elizabeth Newton*. Coxswain Robert Hood received a Bronze Medal for his bravery in this rescue. Parts of the *Doris* can still be seen at certain low tides. Vessels have been beached since then but floated off on the first suitable high tide. The *Anne*, a collier from Holland, was

The wreck of a sailing vessel in 1888 on Seaton beach. The wreck has been exposed from its protective covering of sand for short periods of time over the years. It reappeared in 2003 and has remained visible. It seems that it may not be buried again. This is due, possibly, to changes in the tides. The vessel is thought to be a collier brig and is now protected as an historic wreck site. Pattison's Pictures

driven on to Seaton beach in 1986. People came for miles to see what was once was a common sight.

If the wrecked vessels were on the beach an auction would be held to try and recover some of the loss. Masts, chains, rigging, timber and any cargo that survived could be sold. The remains of a wreck of what is thought to be a nineteenth century brig now lies exposed on Seaton beach when the tide is out. When beached she would have been lying in tons of sand so the timber would have been cut from around the vessel as far down as possible. Occasionally the crew of the lifeboat would be allowed the salvage rights to a vessel.

Breakwaters at Hartlepool and the River Tees were built in the latter part of the nineteenth century causing the sea to retreat from Seaton's coastline and probably saving the village from extinction. The constructions formed a man made bay and made the River Tees easier to navigate. In 1879 these changes caused vast amounts of sand to pile up in the village. The promenade had once been between six and twenty feet above the beach and was now level. It was said that one day there would be nothing left of the village except a church tower sticking out from the sand. Mr Wishart, who was a member of the Hartlepool Port and Harbour Commission and chairman of the Seaton Local Board, remedied the situation before it got out of hand. The sand was levelled out and covered in road scrapings and soil and prairie grass was then planted. This went on year by year until the problem of the sand became manageable. This work was the origin of the green belt along the promenade that we can still see at the present time.

11.3 Lifeboats

If it had not been for the courage and determination of the Seaton and other lifeboat crews the toll of death on this coastline would have been much greater. It was said in the middle of the nineteenth century that the Seaton men could hold their own with any lifeboat crew in Britain. In the early years the station collected a vast amount in charitable contributions, so much in fact, that it was not all spent.

Fishermen would use their own boats in the early rescues, then, in October 1802, Redcar was provided with the *Zetland* and in 1803 Hartlepool received a boat paid for by public subscription. Although these boats performed many rescues between them it was not possible for them to attend every distressed vessel and many a crew was still lost, especially on the notorious Longscar Rocks. That changed due to the generosity of Thomas Backhouse, a Quaker from Sunderland. In 1824 he stood with William Hood, a Seaton pilot, on the beach and they watched helplessly as a vessel was wrecked and the whole crew perished. According to a newspaper account at the time Thomas turned to Will and said: *Dost though think if thou had a lifeboat thou could have saved that crew?* Will answered: *Aye sir, every soul.* Thomas then replied: *Then thou shall have a lifeboat.* Shortly afterwards a lifeboat was sent to Seaton from Sunderland. That first lifeboat was named the *Tees.* A plaque survives that reads

The boathouse, built in 1857, and one of the Charlotte lifeboats, c1870. Author's Collection

'Thomas Backhouse Owner'. It was thought that this plaque was on the boat but there is no record of this being the case. It is more likely that the plaque was attached to the first boathouse that would also have been paid for by Backhouse. A lifeboat station was then established in Seaton by the Tees Bay Lifeboat Association. Thomas Backhouse died shortly after his boat went into service. The Society for the Preservation of Lives in Cases of Shipwreck was formed on 7 January 1825 and at the first meeting held that day at Stockton Town Hall the Seaton lifeboat was one of the main issues. Thomas Backhouse's estate was in the hands of executors of which, his cousin, Jonathan Backhouse (1779–1841) was one. Jonathan agreed to Seaton continuing to use the lifeboat. At the meeting of the Society arrangements were made to have the boat repaired and placed under the care of coxswain William Hood at Jonathan Backhouse's express wish. In 1857, at the request of John Lawson, the RNLI took over the Seaton lifeboat station and a new boat was presented by William McKerrell of Hillhouse, Argyll. The boat was named the *Charlotte* after the donor's wife and had cost £159. In October 1857 a new boathouse was built to the south-west of the site of the old boathouse on land belonging to William Dent. He gave the lifeboat station a fifty year lease on the land. In a letter written in 1877 by Edward Backhouse (1808–1879) the old lifeboat, the *Tees*, was sold for £15 which was donated to the Seaton station. The money was used to build a wall to keep grazing cattle away from the boathouse. Although it is not certain where the *Tees* would have been kept in the twenty years since she was used to save lives it is speculated that she may have been kept for periodical practice or been used on occasion by fishermen.

The Job Hindley lifeboat donated in 1873 in front of the houses on South End and the boathouse built in 1875. Henry Hood, coxswain, and seven members of the crew pose beside the boat, c1885. Author's Collection

On 23 March 1867 the *Charlotte* was taken out for her periodical practice with a crew of eleven. There was a strong wind and the sea was rough so the conditions were perfect to test the abilities of the crew. When the boat was some distance from the shore and in deeper water the waves became more formidable. A large wave washed over the boat and the coxswain, Robert Hood, was pitched into the sea. He was hurriedly dragged back aboard the pitching, water filled boat. The force of trying to row against the strong sea caused four of the oars to snap. The men that were left rowing were unequal to the task of getting the boat to shore. A second large wave washed over the craft and she capsized at an angle. Eight of the crew were thrown into the icy water before the *Charlotte* stabilised. Those left aboard, after an immense struggle, were able to pull their comrades to safety and eventually the boat returned to shore with an unhurt but exhausted group of men. On 25 June 1867 another *Charlotte* was presented to Seaton by the same donor as the first. This *Charlotte* had cost £290 and was larger than the previous one so the boathouse was repaired and altered for the sum of £54. The second *Charlotte* was the first self-righting boat for Seaton. The Superintendent of the Hartlepool Lifeboats was not happy with this new boat. He thought that a flat-bottomed boat would have been more suitable for rescues near rocks, such as Longscar, than the high-floored self-righting model that they had. He wrote in a letter to the Board of Trade that the *Charlotte* was not a lifeboat but a death-boat. His objections must have fallen upon deaf ears because the *Charlotte* served Seaton for six years. In 1873 the *Job Hindley*, costing £323, was donated by its namesake, Job Hindley of Manchester, who had amassed his fortune

Everybody out for the presentation on the Green of the new lifeboat John Lawson in 1888.
Pattison's Pictures

from tripe-dressing. The boat was far too large for the boathouse and had to be stowed outside until a new boathouse was built. Charles Jones, architect, submitted plans in March 1875. The site was to be moved further south-east along the Snook so as to give a better view of the Cleveland Hills from the village. To do this permission had to be obtained from the owners of the land, Lord Eldon and William Dent, before work could begin. This took some time as the owners wished to view the proposed site and the building plans. The boathouse was eventually completed by the builders Ralph Noddings and George Burlinson towards the end of 1876 at a cost for building of £295.6s. Other expenses incurred were for preparing the site by Hartlepool Ironworks. The total cost came to £301. The boathouse was moved again in 1914 when Prisoner's of War built the new road to Port Clarence.

In 1888 a new boat was to be provided from RNLI funds. An argument had raged for some time between the Seaton villagers and the RNLI as to the naming of the boat. The villagers wanted it named after their beloved vicar and honorary secretary for the lifeboat station. The RNLI eventually sent a boat with the name painted on the side. It was the *Mary Isabella*. On 14 February, with great pomp and ceremony, the new boat was placed on a carriage and drawn by six horses down to the beach. John Lawson's granddaughter, Miss Kinnear, christened the boat and James Pattison offered up prayers. The new boat was tested under the watchful eye of

Henry Hood. The villagers, however, were having none of it and still insisted they wanted a boat with their choice of name. The Seaton people won their argument and in May of that year another new boat arrived and the *Mary Isabella* was sent elsewhere. The new boat was drawn by eight horses to the Green where a huge crowd gathered to watch the ceremony. Once again James Pattison called for God's blessing on the boat and her crew. Margaret Lawson then christened the boat after her father, *John Lawson*. The boat was tested by Henry Hood, his crew and members of the Tees Conservancy after which they retired to the *Seven Stars Hotel* to be entertained by the Lifeboat Committee.

In 1906 a temporary boat that belonged to Hartlepool was used. This was the *Charles Ingleby*, built at a cost of £445 and a gift from the Reverend Charles Ingleby's trust fund. The boat was returned to Hartlepool Number 2 Station in 1908.

The *Francis Whitbourn*, costing £802, a gift from Robert Lodge, was placed at Seaton on 28 January 1908 and was in use until early April 1922. On 13 June 1914 a cinemagraph film was made using the *Francis Whitbourn*. In 1907 a motor lifeboat was stationed at the Snook under the care of the Seaton lifeboat station. The boat proved to be expensive as there were breakdowns and it underwent many repairs. There was also the cost of a watchman to look after the boat and it was eventually removed in 1909.

Reverend John Lawson and Henry Hood with the crew and helpers of the John Lawson, 1888. Pattison's Pictures

Until tractors and motorised boats became available horses were used to pull the carriages and very heavy boats out to sea. Sometimes the horses could not be prepared in time and the boat would have to be manually launched which would take much longer. Practices for both horses and men took place at least every quarter. The honorary secretary would have an agreement with the owners of the horses for their use. Most of the rescues took place during the bad weather in the winter months so the farm horses would be more or less idle at those times. In 1918 there was an agreement with Colonel Thomlinson for the use of his horses. A request was sent for them to be brought for practice which was refused by Thomlinson's bailiff. Reverend Beaven, honorary secretary at the time, wrote to Thomlinson to try and sort the matter out. Thomlinson replied that his bailiff felt that the launching took too much out of the horses and he would stand by whatever decision his bailiff made. Correspondence went back and forth on the issue until in August of that year. There must have been bad feeling because Thomlinson, although agreeing to continue his financial support, resigned from the lifeboat committee and could not be persuaded to reconsider his decision.

The cost of the lifeboat going to the assistance of a distressed vessel would be charged to the owner of the vessel wherever possible. All too

The Francis Whitbourne, in service from 1908 to 1922, being pulled down the slipway to the beach by a team of horses. Hartlepool Arts and Museums Collection

often there were circumstances where this could not be done. One case would be if the vessel was wrecked and all hands lost without the vessel being identified. Another was where the owner of a vessel may also be the master and might be drowned. In some cases, where the vessel could be salvaged, either from the rocks or the beach, and sold by auction, the lifeboat crew might be able to claim the salvage to pay for their efforts. The *Porthian* beached in 1869 was one such wreck that was auctioned in 1870 and the proceeds were claimed by the lifeboat crew. Payments for crew, horses, helpers, repairs etc came to a tidy sum and donors were constantly being sought. In the early years much of the funding came from the visiting Quakers. When John Lawson became vicar of Holy Trinity Church in 1835 he also took on the role of honorary secretary to the lifeboat station. He would deal with all the accounts, write to prospective donors and handle all monies received. The succeeding vicars all took on the same role.

By 1920 it was becoming more and more difficult to man the Seaton lifeboat. The real old seafarers had passed away and the succeeding generations were looking for safer work with better wages. In March 1922 the RNLI decided to close the Seaton lifeboat station because it was agreed 'that the crew was a poor one' and it would be financially sensible to have the rescues taken over by the Hartlepool and Teesmouth stations. By April the lifeboat had been sent to London and all the equipment, including the

The SS Clavering when she was wrecked on North Gare near to the Teesmouth on 31 January 1907. This image is from a postcard sent a few days after the event. The writer is commenting that the vessel is breaking up fast and the sea almost covers her at high tide.
Author's Collection

carriage, had been auctioned off at a sale held at Golden Flatts. Only the boathouse remained to be disposed of. Quite a few offers were put forward with different suggestions for its future use, including a cafe. The RNLI asked Reverend Beaven to try and get the highest price possible. After some negotiation and with the intervention of George Vitty, a Town Councillor who had been against the Seaton station closing, the boathouse was to be sold to the West Hartlepool Council for £125 to be used as a shelter in case of rain for children on day trips. The deal was handled by Harry Tilly, solicitor and resident of Church Street in Seaton, and it was found that although the RNLI had owned the boathouse from 1875 they had no deeds for the house or the land. Looking back through earlier documents it would seem that there were never any deeds for the land as it was under lease. However, the council got round this somehow and the sale took place.

The last relic of the Seaton lifeboat station was the barometer that stood near the footpath where the Longscar Hall now stands. Owned by the RNLI 1t had been repaired, repainted blue and a collection box added in 1920. It was decided to leave the barometer for the time being under the care of the West Hartlepool Town Council with the collection box still attached for donations to the RNLI.

11.4 Coxswains

Including the coxswain the crew of a lifeboat usually numbered thirteen, although this was not a hard and fast rule. Throughout the station's 100 year history the crew was made up of fathers, sons and brothers, the same names cropping up again and again throughout the years.

William Hood was the first coxswain and he carried out the task from 1824 until 1 January 1855 when he was succeeded by his son, Robert, who had been a member of the crew. Henry Hood took over as coxswain from Robert Hood on 17 August 1867. Robert Robinson became sub-coxswain in 1870 and resigned twenty-two years later on 22 January 1892 at the age of seventy-five years. John Franklin then became sub-coxswain. Henry Hood retired as coxswain after thirty-one years in 1898 with James Edward Lithgo becoming sub-coxswain and John Henry Franklin becoming coxswain until resigning on 16 July 1909 due to ill health. James Lithgo took the position of coxswain from 1909 until his death on 21 July 1911. At the age of twenty-seven, John Lithgo became coxswain after him and George Storer was promoted to sub-coxswain. In 1918 John Lithgo handed in his resignation but was persuaded to stay on, which he did for another two years. In 1920 William Lithgo was offered the position but he turned it down and Robert Henry Bulmer was appointed and remained as coxswain until the closure of the station in 1922.

On 30 October 1851 William Hood was voted the Silver Medal for, along with his crew, going to the rescue of thirty-two vessels and assisting in

Henry Hood, coxswain of the Seaton lifeboats from 1867 to 1898. Hartlepool Arts and Museums Collection

saving 120 lives. Robert Hood was voted the RNLI Silver medal in 1863 for his long service.

On 2 May 1883 Henry Hood, Matthew and John Henry Franklin were voted the RNLI Silver Medal for going to the assistance of the schooner

Atlas when she ran aground on 11 March 1883. Reverend John Lawson gave the awards at the Seaton Carew vicarage in the presence of the local lifeboat committee and dignitaries of the village. They were also presented with a framed record of their achievement signed by the Duke of Northumberland, who was president of the RNLI. Queen Victoria also conferred the Albert Medal second class on Henry Hood for his bravery on the same occasion. On Henry Hood's retirement he was voted a second silver clasp to his Silver Medal. In a room of the National School in Ashburn Street, Reverend CB Hunter presented Hood with the clasp, certificate of service, silver watch, gold chain and a grant of £62 from the RNLI. He was also presented with a purse containing £30 which had been given by the committee and crew of the lifeboat.

In 1907 John Henry Franklin was awarded a second silver clasp to his Silver Medal for services to the *SS Clavering* when she went aground on 1 January that year. On a total of four attempts at rescue, twenty-six of the crew were taken of by the Seaton temporary lifeboat, *Charles Ingleby*, and eighteen by the Hartlepool boat. Nineteen of the crew of sixty-three were lost. Salvage rights for the vessel were given in January 1908.

In the early days of the Seaton lifeboat records were kept but they were often just pencilled accounts on scraps of paper. From 1857, when the RNLI took over the station, careful logs, known as Return of Wreck, were kept by the coxswain every time the lifeboat was launched. The records that survive from the nineteenth century tell harrowing tales and also tales of great bravery by the men who risked their lives every time they faced the fierce North Sea in, by today's standards, what was a very flimsy craft which competed against some of nature's worst elements to save the lives of their fellow man.

Chapter Twelve

As a Resort

There are few recorded links between the fourteenth and eighteenth centuries except for births, deaths and perpetual quarrels over land and rights. The records began again in the late eighteenth century when there were vast changes to the sleepy little village. Quakers from Darlington and Sunderland, mainly wealthy bankers, wanted somewhere to go during the summer away from the pressure of their work and Seaton was ideal. The villagers, from being farmers and fisher-folk, suddenly became adept at catering for visitors. Besides the *New Inn* and its attendant lodging houses, every house and cottage in the village that had one or more rooms to spare took in paying guests. In 1812 William Tate described the village:

Looking north from Mrs Burton's shop with the barometer to the front of the view. In the centre of the row of houses is the Seven Stars. The old cannon lies by the side of the footpath as if someone has just abandoned it. A group of boys and men stand talking in the road. One of the boys is carrying a big bass fiddle so perhaps the boys have just had a music lesson, 1888. Pattison's Pictures

A watering place of high estimation, families of the first consequence, the peer, the prelate, the knight and the esquire, resort to Seaton. In fact no place can be more conveniently situated for sea-bathing; the salubrity of the air, the hospitable treatment, the cleanliness of the place, the great length of level sand (extending from the Teesmouth to Hartlepool) together with the snook (which stretches from the village to the river Tees, quite even and without obstruction; and covered with a fine verdure, on which feed numerous herds of cattle and sheep) all greatly contribute to the gratification of the visitant.

Tate goes on to tell us that there were about sixty houses in the village at this time, many of them in use for taking paying guests. There were two hot baths and one cold shower bath, plenty of fresh produce, in the form of sea-food, meat, vegetables and hot bread. Amusements consisted of pleasure sailing, shell-collecting, horse riding, Jack bowls and quoits. Two thirds of the villagers were employed as waiters, cooks, laundresses and cleaners etc.

The records for the next fifty years or so are rather sparse but the village certainly remained popular with the Darlington visitors. Bathing machines, copied from the new invention being used on the beaches at

Children posing on the beach. From left to right: Young Lumley, Ralph and Fred Mullins, Vitty, Lillian Hogg, Lumley. The little boy in the sailor's cap has his back turned and seems to be oblivious to what's happening behind him, 1887. Pattison's Pictures

Scarborough, were introduced to protect the modesty of those wishing to sample the delights of the sea. In 1842 the 'civil and industrious' bathing machine attendant was Mary. It was her job to 'dip' the ladies and the children, a task she carried out for more than thirty years. Billiard tables were introduced and the beach was used for walking, horse riding, shell collecting and playing croquet.

By the late 1860s Redcar had become fashionable and had lured the visitors away from Seaton so the Local Board decided it was time to give the village a face-lift and they began to carry out improvements. During these improvements in 1869 Seaton did not look its best. The promenade was being extended to the south and there were earthworks everywhere. The wreck of the *Porthian* was on the beach described as being like '*the half clothed ribs of a yet unseen sea-serpent, uncanny and weird in the extreme*'. In October of that year a special correspondent from the *London Times* was visiting Saltburn. On the advice of a friend he detoured through Seaton on his way back to London, spending about three hours in the village. His later description was that, although he did not stay long enough to form more than a superficial impression, he thought Seaton was primitive and

Pattison's caption 'Showing how it's done'. The same group of children as in the previous image inspecting a camera. Someone had to be taking this photo. Is it possible the camera may have belonged to Francis Frith and Pattison could have been taking the photo or vice versa? 1887. Pattison's Pictures

The Garbutt family, coal merchants, enjoying a trip in their coble the Jubilest, 1888.
Pattison's Pictures

looked like a village that had somehow strayed to the sea-side and was too bashful to assume the conventional maritime air. There was only one old fashioned hotel but the village boasted the kind of shops that sell everything from sealing-wax to second hand coffins. He thought that the landladies of the village were at least a generation behind their sisters of more enlightened places in the nineteenth century art of extortion. His advice was that he would recommend it as an admirable place for retreat for anyone weary of the gay or busy world. The correspondent's advice must have been heard because in that year Thomas Walker built his mansion and other buildings soon followed erected by magistrates, doctors, ship-owners and other businessmen and professionals. Many of the larger houses along Station Lane were built at this time and a few years later the large houses on Front Street facing the sea were erected.

By 1870 Seaton had picked up considerably, not only because of improvements in the erection of a new sea wall and gas lamps lighting the promenade, but because Redcar had an outbreak of smallpox and was being avoided. The gas for the new lamps was brought by mains from the Hartlepool Gas and Water Works. This was due to Mr West, the pioneer of gas to dozens of towns and villages in the north of England, and to Mr Davidson who saw them installed in Seaton. Mr West was a resident of Seaton and a grand party was held in his house on the Green to celebrate

Paddling from a coble. The bathing machines are ready for work and there is a swimmer to the right of the view, 1888. Pattison's Pictures

Ladies with their offspring in perambulators head towards the bathing machines to prepare for a dip, 1888. Pattison's Pictures

the introduction of this essential commodity. A new footpath was laid from Station Lane to South End paid for by the Local Board. The residents were asked to asphalt from their houses to the path at their own expense, which they happily agreed to do. William Charles Ward Jackson donated a drinking fountain, which received pride of place by replacing the old stocks that were by the roadside on the Green. Fishing trips in the little cobles would render a harvest of whiting, gurnet and haddock. Lodging houses and the hotel were full. Three greengrocers carried their wares about on carts ready to cut each other's throats in genial competition. The only objectionable thing in the village was said to be a fish-cart that carried some terrible looking monsters of the deep. In July 1873 a reporter for the *South Durham Herald* wrote a very descriptive article on a walk he took around the village. He mentions his starting point as being the old-fashioned hall known as Carr House with the lighthouse nearby. He stands in front of Staincliffe House with his mouth open in awe at the ingenuity of man in the erection of the mansion surrounded by kitchen gardens, lawns, conservatories and a long wall, that was perhaps built to stop the encroaches of the sea. Adjoining Staincliffe House is the Old Hall Garth with its original draw well and a small portion of its old moat. A row of dilapidated cottages follows and, on the left of these, an old property belonging to the Backhouse family, at present in the occupation of a Jack of all trades local character, known commonly as Fat Jack. The sign outside the property states: *R Robinson, fruiterer, greengrocer, licensed to sell tea, coffee, tailor, paperhanger and carpet maker, also the village crier and coal*

Men in straw boaters take a casual stroll past the drinking fountain and the barometer. A little group seems to have a table set up and be indulging in a picnic near to the bandstand, c1920. Author's Collection

merchant. On the Green the writer notes that the dragon has lost its lair and the king his crown. He is referring to the *George and Dragon* and the *King's Head Inns* both having now become private residences. Many of the other large houses around the square are in use as schools. On walking up Station Lane he comments on some of the buildings and beautiful gardens that stand side by side with old cottages. Thomas Walker had started a trend that continued in the erection of some grand and substantial houses. The railway station the writer describes as being open and uncomfortable. Returning to the main road, the writer mentions the *Seaton Hotel* now in the hands of Harry Thornton. The previously dilapidated hotel has been completely refurbished through the new landlord's efforts. Harry Thornton's son also has a hand in the modernisation of the village by running a conveyance called the Southern Fly which was a convenient form of transport throughout the village. What was known later as the Royal Café was a formidable building erected in the late eighteenth century. In 1873 it was occupied by J Lister, Buoy House manager for the Tees Conservancy. Next to this large house was the postoffice. The back street, Ashburn Street, housed the National School, the Temperance Hall and the reading room. The village had four butchers, four grocers and as many shoemakers and tailors. Once again the lodging houses were full. Charles Lamb and Mary were sweeping out and carpeting the bathing machines while the proprietor, Humbleby, was rubbing his hands in glee at the prospect of a good season. Lists of visitors, published weekly in the papers throughout the summer season, showed that people were travelling to Seaton from as far away as London. By 1874 there were plans to build a pier just to the south of the Green and a fifty-roomed hotel in the hope that this would lure visitors away from Redcar. Sadly it was not to be, as still so often happens in Seaton the plans came to nothing. Money was scarce at this time due to a depression in the iron-works and it was found that the finance for these grand ventures could not be procured.

1876 saw the road southward of the Green widened and a sea-wall being erected. A row of dilapidated houses at the north end of the village were knocked down and removed. Most of the work was done using local labour and materials to keep the cost down. The Local Board covered some of the cost and the rest was raised by public subscription of about £200. July of 1879 brought a newspaper report in which the benefits of Seaton were expounded. The Snook, with its pleasantly positioned, wide-open spaces was being used by the auxiliary forces for field-days and rifle competitions. Galas, both religious and otherwise, were also held on the Snook. In 1905 a new promenade was completed. In 1926 the promenade extension from the *Staincliffe* to Station Lane and the South and North Shelters were completed at a cost of £42,000. Except for the war years the village continued with its popularity as a resort well into the twentieth century. Instead of paying guests staying for weeks at a time, with transport readily available and distances seemingly becoming shorter, the visitors became mainly day-trippers. They would step off the train in their

A busy day on the beach. George Siddle's Star Café will be doing a roaring trade, c1935.
Author's Collection

hundreds and swarm, like a black mass, down Station Lane. By 1938 they were arriving in buses and coaches and alighting at the new bus station.

In about 1930 George Siddle saw the potential for a thriving business in Seaton. He set up merry-go-rounds, a chairoplane and other rides. He had a café called the Star and other kiosks and obtained sole rights to rent beach sites to icecream salesmen, donkey keepers and others wishing to

The devastation to Siddle's fairground equipment after a freak spring tide, c1935. Courtesy of George Colley

A travelling fair that has set up its rides on the beach. This is probably in the 1940s.
Author's Collection

hawk their wares. Siddle also acquired the fish shop that is now Bees. He lived at and ran his little empire from number 4 The Front. During freak spring tides one year, just as he was setting his rides up for the season, his equipment was badly damaged by the water. During the Second World War, George had to move his little fairground further away from the beach as it was a restricted zone. In the 1940s the council asked for tenders from anyone wishing to rent the large area of land beside the beach at the south end of Seaton. By this time John Collins, who came from Wales, had arrived on the scene. He put forward a larger tender than George and Collins' fairground was set up. By the time George retired in the1950s he no longer had fairground rides but still had shops. The business was handed over to his daughter, Dorothy, and her husband, who carried on the running of the shops until the late 1980s. George was perhaps a bit of a rough diamond but was an astute businessman and was always looking at property around the sea front. Because of this habit he acquired the nickname 'The Mayor of Seaton'. George died in 1987 at the age of 87 leaving behind him fond memories of wonderful summers in those who had been children in the twenty or so years that his enterprises had given pleasure.

Collins' fairground had, besides the usual merry-go-rounds and rides, a large wooden Ferris wheel. Local children were paid a little pocket money to man the stalls. In its heyday the fairground would be packed and ice-cream and hot-dog vendors would do a thriving trade. The vendors would put in a tender to the council for a parking spot. The highest tenders would get the best sites. These would be on the green belt between the

The Front, Seaton Carew

The paddling pool and roller skating rink in 1973. Author's Collection

beach and the road or just round from the bus station where they would get people passing on their way to and from the fairground. By the 1980s health and safety regulations were becoming stricter and the little fairgrounds were going out of fashion as other forms of entertainment took their place. Eventually the fairground closed and the equipment was dismantled. This marked the end of an era for the people who had been children in those years.

A tiny Swan China cooking pot on sale to tourists in the 1960s. The pot is embellished with the Seaton crest of a crown, three lions and a sturgeon. The Author

Chapter Thirteen

The Wars

In 1902, to celebrate the end of the Boer War, bonfires were lit on three sand dunes that stood where the slipway from Station Lane goes down to the beach. The dunes were named Ladysmith, Mafeking and Spion Kop.

The Mascots were a popular group of entertainers that often performed at the Seaton Carew bandstand situated on the sea-front. In August 1914, less than an hour before they were due to perform, war was declared between Britain and Germany. In December of the same year there was a bombardment of Hartlepool and Seaton. A few days later there was a Zeppelin scare. The military took over the golf course and for three years the only people to actually play golf were the high ranking officials from the Yorkshire Regiment.

There were two airfields at Seaton Carew, both beginning service after the formation of the Home Defence squadrons in 1916. One was an area of about 72 acres and was situated just to the south of Hunter House Farm. It comprised an aeroplane shed, two hangers, stores, huts, power house and other buildings. There were also bomb stores both above and below ground. The other was a seaplane station and was adjacent to where the power station is now. This airfield was over an area of about seven acres with a seaplane shed, two hangers and a few other buildings. Part of the slipway still remains. Soon after the war the buildings were dismantled and the sites abandoned. There are records of at least five ships sinking between 1914 and 1918 through being torpedoed or detonating mines just out to sea between Redcar and Hartlepool.

On the night of 27 November 1916 Second Lieutenant LV Pyott took off from Seaton Carew to find a Zeppelin that had been spotted by the Hutton Henry searchlight. He soon sighted the airship and followed it for about five miles firing at every opportunity. After firing seventy-one rounds the German airship caught fire and fell into the sea off West Hartlepool. Pyott's face was burned by the heat of the wreckage. The airship had done some damage before it was blown from the sky. It had dropped sixteen bombs as it passed over West Hartlepool. Four people were killed and thirty-four injured. Another plane that took off from Seaton Carew at the same time failed to return with its crew of two men. In 1918 ten Blackburn Kangaroo planes were operating out of Seaton Carew. Between 1 May and the armistice on 11 November they flew over the North Sea on convoy protection. When the Armistice was declared all the Blackburn Kangaroos were put up for sale at Seaton Carew where they were all sold, mainly for commercial purposes. In 1920 converted military aircraft gave pleasure flights from Seaton Carew for 5s (25p). In February 1921 a small cross was

The ten bi-planes that attracted huge crowds when they landed on the beach in 1914. The planes belonged to the number 2 flying squad of the Royal Flying Corps and were flying in short hops from Montrose to Salisbury Plain in Wiltshire. A large white cross was placed on the beach as a landing marker. At this time there were the rumblings of the start of a World War. Author's Collection

unveiled on the Green. It is a memorial to the 23 men from Seaton who lost their lives and to give thanks for the safe return of 203 men and 9 women. On the same day a new clock and four bells were installed in the church tower. These were given by Colonel Thomlinson and his wife, Hannah, in commemoration of the war dead.

In June 1940 the beach and promenade were sealed off with barbed wire and mined as a coastal defence. There was no access to the beach for the general public. Road blocks were set up and drivers and pedestrians were stopped and questioned about their movements. George Siddle's roundabout, near the beach slipway at the bottom of Station Lane, was requisitioned and used as camouflage over a concrete pillbox. Many of the large houses and hotels were taken over by the military to be used for accommodation. The swimming baths were closed to the public and used as an army barracks. A large portion of the golf course was also fenced off. Barbed wire was strung up, anti-tank blocks sunk, landmines set and concrete blockhouses erected. However, due to a sympathetic military command only three holes were out of bounds. On 26 August eleven high explosive bombs fell on the Snook. In June 1941 Thomas Cowan, a pupil at Seaton School was playing with his pals. He ran onto the golf course and was killed by a mine exploding. In March 1943 incendiaries were dropped on the Snook.

An underground radar station was opened in Brenda Road. Two searchlight batteries were in place where the junction of Swainby and Stokesly Road is now. Another searchlight and a Lewis gun site were situated by a pond in a field just opposite Glentower Grove, Bransdale Grove now covers the site. The Seaton Carew Royal Observer Corp post was situated near the golf course on the coast road opposite to where the Mayfair Centre is now. The post was underground and had a crew of about ten, some from Seaton. The Chief Observer was Reg Williams. All the members were male and of all ages over sixteen. They would do shifts with a crew of three or four at a time. Their uniform was blue with a navy blue beret and their badge was an Elizabethan beacon lighter with the motto 'Forewarned is Forearmed'. The post closed in 1968.

On 2 October 1941 a German aircraft dropped four bombs on Seaton. One landed in Eggleston's farmyard which was opposite the Co-operative stores on Station Lane. Two came down in North Road, one of which landed on a garage throwing a car over the top of the houses to land near the North Shelter. Another landed on the south-west corner of the Green. Windows were blown out of the houses nearby and the roof of number 7 Green Terrace collapsed. A dip in the path on the Green still marks the spot where the bomb landed. There were some injuries sustained but no fatalities except for the poor chickens from the farmyard. Bombs also fell on the zinc works causing considerable damage to buildings. Near to the railway station Spitfires brought down a drifting barrage balloon before its trailing cables caused any damage.

The War Memorial situated on the north-east corner of the Green. Courtesy of George Colley

In 1945 the beach was once again opened to the public. The rides were set in motion and the donkeys trotted up and down the beach with their small charges. In 1968 a mortar shell was discovered in a bunker on the golf course, an overlooked relic from the war.

Chapter Fourteen

Graciosa

The following story was published in a broadsheet in the nineteenth century. The places are real and where the names of people have been recorded in documents of the era I have added dates. Although real surnames from families in the area at that time have been used, the main players in the story and the events are fictitious. The tale is set in Blackhall and Hartlepool and does not directly relate to Seaton Carew. Its inclusion is due to the fact that it was written by John Lawson, the vicar of Seaton, and is part of the Pattison collection along with images that relate specifically to the story. It also paints a vivid picture of life on the north-east coast in the eighteenth century which I hope readers find interesting.

The ruined cottage at Blackhall that once belonged to Mrs Gray and her two sons. Pattison's Pictures

Graciosa
By J Lawson

The line of coast extending northwards from the mouth of the River Tees to Seaham and Bishop Wearmouth is so pretty and so pleasantly diversified in character that it seems odd that it should have escaped description. It may be well that it is so: for perhaps the best thing that can happen to those of us who love quiet, in these uneasy days of travel, is to have the beauties of our own particular neighbourhood left unsung.

Certainly, in the last century, the little port of Hartlepool and the huge limestone caverns of Blackhall, which lie some few miles further north, were visited by one who was among Englishmen to observe and describe the beauties of natural scenery, the poet Thomas Gray (1716–1771) writing in 1765:

> 'I have been for two days in Hartlepool to taste the waters, and do assure you that nothing could be salter, and bitterer and nastier, and better for you. I am delighted with the place. There are the finest walks and rocks and caverns and dried fishes, and all manner of small inconveniences a man can wish'.

And again, to another correspondent, he writes a little later on:

One of the rock formations at Blackhall known by locals as the Lonesome. This was demolished early this year (2004) because it had become unstable. Pattison's Pictures

*'The rocks, the sea, and the weather, these more than made up to me the want
of bread and the want of water, two capital defects, but of which I learned
from the inhabitants not to be sensible. They live on the refuse of their own
fish market, with a few potatoes and a reasonable quantity of geneva,
(bootleg gin) six days in the week, and I have nowhere seen a taller, more
robust, healthy race; every house full of ruddy broad-faced children; nobody
dies but of drowning and old age'.*

Things are sadly changed there since then, no doubt; but even now, so long
after, the description holds good in great measure. The ruddy children, the
caves and rocks, the hardy pilots, the dried cod, and the geneva are all still
there, pretty much as they were when seen by the poet, in the early days
of good old King George III. (1760–1820)

At the time of our story they were in the full swing of their untarnished
glory; and to the delights of geneva were added those of cognac and
tobacco, openly landed and freely dispensed by smugglers. The narrow
chares and wynds swarmed to overflow with troops of sturdy bare-legged
urchins. A maze of clothes-lines bespanned the crooked ways, oilskins and
jerseys fluttering gaily aloft in the brisk rush of east wind as it swept
madly up some blind alley or funnel-like cul-de-sac. Gay petticoats hung
dependant from man in attic window, while in the lane below was a merry
and ceaseless babble of divers tongues and languages.

> *And on the broken pavement, here and there,*
> *Doth many a stinking sprat and herring lie:*
> *A brandy and tobacco shop is near,*
> *And hens and dogs and hogs are feeding by:*
> *And here a sailor's jacket hangs to dry.*
> *At every door are sunburnt matrons seen*
> *Mending old nets to catch the scaly fry.*

The year 1740 was remarkable for atmospheric disturbances. It came in with
a frost, the like of which had not been known in England for thirty-one years:
a frost of such great strength that the Thames was frozen over, and of such
long continuance that a man, writing on 17 April, says *'This day, for the first
time, spirits rose to the point of warmth'*. What his spirits were, and what his
point of warmth, I know not; but whatever their precise meaning, his remark
points evidently to prolonged and unusual cold. Violent and destructive
thunderstorms marked the course of the summer, from beginning to end.
November was ushered in bygone of the most furious and fatal gales of the
century. Between Boston and Lynn sixty ships and upwards lay wrecked. At
Whitby, the damage done both at sea and ashore was incredible; and from
the Firth to Forth to the mouth of the Thames, there was scarce a port or a
fishing village escaped without damage and the loss of life.

The morning of All Saints (1 November) broke mild and calm,
unusually so for the time of year and all Hartlepool was early astir; as

today they were to celebrate the capture of Portobello (November 1739) by Admiral Edward Vernon and the return to their homes of four young townsmen who had taken a part in that gallant action on board Captain Thomas Trevor's ship, the *Stratford.*

The revels were led by Mr John Hedworth, who had ridden in overnight from his house in the country, to do honour to the town of which he was mayor, (mayor from 1716–1740) and grace the feast with his presence. Till noon all went merrily enough and the crowd was gathered on the town moor to see the roasting of an ox. Dense columns of smoke from the crackling faggots shot straight up into the thick autumnal haze. Low sunshine lay on sea and land; belated gnats and midges dancing gaily up and down in the grateful rays. Yet, for all this, old tars and weather-wise salts bent their gaze steadily seaward and rumour soon had it that a storm was at hand. Nor was rumour far wrong; for half an hour later the blazing fire was extinguished by a deluge of icy rain, and of that great throng on the moor, all were swept away before the fury of the blast, to seek shelter in low-lying streets and closes, at the back of the town wall by the little pilot pier. Not one soul now of them remained on the moor, but only the poor half-roasted, half-sodden ox, creaking and swinging on his spit, like some highwayman in his gibbet chains. So lately the idol and hope of the mob, now a forgotten and forsaken cinder!

In the town below, men dodged the flying slates and tiles; and hardy women, beshawled and hooded, stood out in sheltered nooks, to see the swirl of the tide and the chance of a wreck. Wrecks, in that day, possessing an interest they have quite lost in this. For with the actual excitement and flurry of the event was then ever mixed anticipation of blessings in store. Salvation of life was the last thing thought of, a cargo of French brandy was perhaps the first. But if brandy was not forthcoming, why, then they would do with sherry, and sherry sure enough they did with that day. For a Spanish brigantine flew in before the hurricane, out of the darkness and spindthrift seawards, and in ten minutes after she was first sighted, had dashed herself to pieces on the cruel ridge of rock at the harbour mouth. Down ran the rummaging, ransacking mob; rifling the dead and dying, and falling with a fury like that of the storm itself, on all they could lay hold of. Their greed of drink was insatiable. Of one man it is handed down to this day that, pulling off his trousers and tying them up at the waist, he dipped them in a broached sherry cask, and bore them off in triumph over his back, full inflated like the pig-skin of a wine seller!

What an ending to a day so auspiciously begun! What a miserable scene of degradation: men, dead-drunk, lying helpless among men really dead! For these last, slain in manful combat with the sea, small pity was shown. But for the sots who lay among them, their comrades did show some care, hauling them up out of harm's way, above reach of the flowing tide. And there they were left in the darkness and drift, to recover their reason and their legs.

Of all the vessel's company, battered and broken by the flinty rock, but one was found alive, and that one a woman. She was dying fast, when they

Sandwell Chare, where Phoebe Pounder, Graciosa's foster mother, had her little shop.
Pattison's Pictures

came across her in the gloom of early night; and hastily snatching a shutter from the nearest shop-door, young men carried her up to old Phoebe Pounder's in Sandwell Chare, close by the water-gate of the wall, below which she had been flung ashore. The gossips stood round in groups by the closet-bed in which they laid her. It was a scene after their own hearts, and one not readily to be foregone, mystery, a death, and a birth, all in one!

They sent word to Mr Hugh Petrie, (Reverend D H Petrie-wife Mary buried 10 July 1794 in St Hilda's Churchyard) the curate of the town, to bring the consolation of his office; but the poor castaway never regained consciousness; and long before his arrival, was gone softly down to the House of Silence and carrying her secret with her. All it remained for him to do was name the infant, so untowardly born into this troublesome world, and so quickly forsaken. They called her *Graciosa*, after the ship that had brought her there, and whose name they had found on a piece of painted wreckage. Under the fostering care of the good woman, into whose charge her dying mother had been given, the little one grew into a fine, frolicsome child, and gave early promise of great beauty.

When no more than three years old, her foster mother, with her family and the little *Graciosa*, moved to Coniscliffe, to take charge of a squalid farm belonging to Mr Jennison, of which generations of Pounders, or their relatives, the Hunters, had been tenants time out of mind. Here they managed to exist till the early days of the year 1746, when their homestead was pillaged by some camp-followers in the train of Marshal George Wade, (1673–1748) who, with his army, passed over Pierce Bridge, hurrying north to Culloden.

After this they led a hard, joyless life of penury and toil, still clinging with true conservative tenacity to the impoverished acres, till May 1749, when a strange disease that broke suddenly out among horned cattle in the County Palatine, completed their ruin.

Even so, it was with sorrow and many a long, lingering look behind, they wrenched themselves away from the miserable spot: the sons going as hinds to a yeoman at Elstob, and Phoebe (with her young charge) finding her way by waggon back to Hartlepool, a poorer woman than the day she left it.

She now set up a little shop in one of the narrow chares that lead out of the High Street seawards, in the selfsame house; in fact, she had quitted six years before. The parish priest recommended her to the flock saying '*I commend unto you Phoebe, our sister, that ye receive her as becometh saints, and that ye assist her in whatsoever business she hath need of you;*' and being a decent, civil body, and moreover a native, she found excellent custom

The Fish Sands and the town wall at Hartlepool where, as a child, Graciosa would watch the fishermen. Pattison's Pictures

among her neighbours and the sea-faring men of the place, and years slipped not altogether unprosperously by.

At fifteen years of age *Graciosa* had sprung up into a tall and sprightly lass; good to gaze on, with those drooping eyelids which are so irresistibly bewitching, and which, I verily believe, have wrought more havoc among mankind than every other female grace and charm.

Her beauty, of course, was but in the bud, her diablerie (sorcery) and espieglerie (frolicsomeness) in full bloom. They were not of a sort that had any great malignancy about them, or betokened badness of heart; but proceeded in part from excess of animal spirits and exuberant health, and partly (no doubt) from the unhappy fact that she had the grave misfortune to run her little race before the invention of that crown and glory of our own enlightened age, Board Schools. Hence it happened that, except when helping old Phoebe about the shop and house, time lay pretty much at her own disposal; and she spent more of it than was meet on the sea-wall, in gossip with other girls in their teens, or in idle badinage with the fisher-lads mending their herring nets on the sandy beach below. These last stood her pert chaff and pretty pranks, the well aimed pebble, the hurtling log or dancing chip, the nut of offence and

A rock formation that stood at Hartlepool. Known as Elephant Rock it collapsed on 10 May 1891. At low tide the 'feet' are still visible. Pattison's Pictures

apple of wanton provocation, with stolid good humour, in a general way:
their hearts pierced by the shafts of her ready wit and (if truth must needs
be told) their faces not infrequently damaged by her Amazonian
onslaughts. For she *'set at naught the frivolous bolt of Cupid,'* and if any of
the lads were inclined to be saucy, or essayed to carry his advances
beyond a decent bound, the girl stood quickly on the defensive, nay, did
not scruple to engage in active hostilities, and carry the warfare briskly
into the enemy's camp.

Her pert airs and arch ways not withstanding, the girl was truly feminine
and lovable; plump and soft with a tender heart, and cherry lips waiting to
be kissed. Not that she knew all this, nor ever once thought about herself
and her charms; but so it was, and the destined day was not very far distant
when poor *Graciosa* was to understand it all, and to find her fate.

Meanwhile, two more years of rollicking life and hoydenish ways sped
quickly by, without much mark or record; humble household duties
dividing her care with banter on the sea-wall, and airy moonlight romps
on the town moor. Tales of smuggling had risen to an alarming and
unprecedented height. Troops of soldiers and sailors, set free by the peace
of Aix-la-Chapelle, (18 October 1748) scoured the kingdom, destitute, left
by an ungrateful country to their hard fate. Very many of them, from sheer
lack of worthier employment, turned smugglers; and their doings became
a terror to all peaceable and law-abiding citizens. Hanged they were, no
doubt, by scores, as any one may see for himself, who cares to glance at the
new-letters of the day. But as fast as they hanged one batch, another arose,
more hardy and daring than the last.

And, moreover, the barbarous severity of the law enlisted, ere long, the
goodwill and sympathy of the multitude on behalf of these lawless men,
so that they became difficult to catch, and the aid of preventive men and
common informers was used to entrap them. These informers had but a
short shrift if they fell into the toils of the smugglers, nor did they stand
high in favour with the natives of those ports at which their stations lay. In
proof whereof, give ear to a corroborative incident that occurred in
Hartlepool just at this time.

A gang of notorious smugglers, who had long infested the Blackhall rocks,
finding in those desolate, sea-washed caverns convenient stowage for their
contraband goods, had word sent them that a preventive man was come
down and on the look-out. The captain of the smugglers was one Trollop; he,
his son Jerry, and some of their mates, disguised as rustics, sallied out into the
town, and picking acquaintance with the unsuspecting spy, plied him with
drink at a tavern. Pouncing on their prey when half-seas over, they bound
him hand and foot, carried him down in broad daylight to a boat at the pier-
head, and shipped him aboard a ketch bound for Helvoetsluys (Holland).
The man was no more seen in Hartlepool, and the feat of the smugglers met
with applause on all hands, as a just and glorious revenge.

Perched high above the Blackhall rocks, on a wind-swept table-land,
stood (and still stands) a lonely farm looking out onto the restless ocean.

Its octagon dovecot, rising like some donjon keep from the very verge of the crag, still makes a notable beacon for such mariners that pass that way. A stone's throw north of house and dovecot, three forlorn larches, bowed double under prevalence of cutting easterly gales, stretch their gaunt arms westward, for all the world like witches on a blasted heath.

Here dwelt, in the days of our story, a widow woman, who with her two sons, Peter and Leonard Gray, managed the steading in an old-fashioned way; their thrift and diligence often thwarted and frustrated by the cold sour clay and unkindly climate.

The smugglers in the caves down below were a constant source of anxiety and worry to the poor widow. Not that she feared their violence or malice, far from it. Her fear was lest the young men, her sons, should become involved in some hazardous enterprise. There seems no question, but that both the lads were on a friendly footing with Trollop, even to the extent of visiting his caves and secret stores; but there is no evidence forthcoming that their dealings with the gang went beyond a little very natural barter of goods, a sack of coarse-ground oatmeal occasionally finding its way down to the shore, while a bottle of cognac, with a parcel of tea and tobacco, would cheer the inmates of the house above.

Peter and his brother, Lennie, were well-known figures in Hartlepool, where they came almost weekly, wind and weather permitting, on marketing errands, in their little cockle-shell of a boat. Old Phoebe's shop was their common house of call; and while his brother was on the shingle below, loading their boat for their homeward trip, Peter would linger long at the counter, unable to tear himself away from the sweet *Graciosa*.

As time wore on and the boating trips followed one another with still increasing frequency, the widowed mother grew more troubled and suspicious than ever, especially when she observed in how silent and preoccupied a mood her eldest son now invariably returned from his voyages.

Little kenned she of the magnet that drew her Peter's shallop with such sure and sweet attraction to the shop in Sandwell Chare. She felt sure that some dire secret lay deep within his breast; and yet, with the fear of those desperadoes down below ever before her, she durst not ask or seek to know it, but passed her days, during the lad's absence, in nervous misery and heartache.

One September evening, rheumatic old Phoebe Pounder, crutch at hand, sat by the fireside knitting. A cosy cat, coiled in the old dame's lap, purred in warm approval of the situation. The kettle on the hob sent forth its jets of spouting steam with quick petulant clicks of clattering lid. Rashers of ham spluttered and frizzled in their frying pan hard by. The knitting needles glinting in the glow of sea-coal flame, clinked with a sort of rhythmic cadence. The solemn clock behind the parlour door, in slow and measured tones, told the hour of eight; and *Graciosa*, rousing from some pleasant fancy, bestirred herself to close the shop and lay the cloth, when Peter Gray's well known footfall echoed on the pavement without. In he came hale and ruddy from the crisp sea air, *'Oh Peter! You stupid boy, how late you are again!'* was *Graciosa's* greeting *'The hour of sale is past, the shop is closed. Why <u>have</u> you been so long?'*

That last was surely a pleasant sentence to hear, that emphasis on <u>have</u> from the lips of the girl he loved. Perhaps the young man knew what he was about (and *Graciosa* too) in thus putting off his visit till the shop should be closed and he could have the girl to himself, without the interruption of stray customers and prying eyes.

'Never mind Peter my lad. You know the girl's saucy ways. Come in and welcome' cried old Phoebe from her chair. *'The moon is full; plenty o' time to share our bit supper. Draw up to the table my lad and fall to'.*

The bashful Peter, nothing loath, did as he was bid and drew up and perhaps no cheerier little supper party was to be found in all Hartlepool that night. But the sweetest hour on earth must have its end and the clock's first stroke of nine, with Lennie's shrill whistle of impatience from the beach below, fell harshly and full soon on love-sick Peter's ear.

'Oh but Gracie,' said he, turning back when he had gained the doorway *'I must have some sweets for the old mother at home'.* That doling out of sweets can be made to take an unconscionable time: 'tis long before some customers are suited to their mind, and Lennie's whistles rose from shrill to shriller.

Rough seas battering the town wall at Hartlepool. Pattison's Pictures

'*Come Peter, wish the girl goodnight and be off, there's a man: don't keep that lad waiting any longer out in the cold, you've a long pull back and your old mother'll be worriting herself to death'*. Poor Peter still seemed to hesitate and a silvery voice came back from the shop,' "*Oh Peter, Peter! What a great baby you are! Hardbake, butter scotch, mint drops, treacle toffy, barley sugar, sugar candy and now liquorice and Spanish juice for the old woman! I know right well Lennie and you will eat them all up in the boat. I thought it was only boys who cared for sweets!*'

'*Ah Gracie, Gracie*' cried old Phoebe Pounder peering at the pretty pair over the rim of her horn spectacles. '*Ah Gracie, my poor innocent, was there ever a young man yet that didn't care for sweets?*'

That shrewd fireside remark brought all conversation to an abrupt close. The young man held the door ajar, latch in hand, apparently in the very act of going. But no; they must needs have whispered words on the very threshold, till Phoebe, chilled past all patience, called out at the top of her voice, '*Shut that door and begone, and you Gracie, come in this very minute*', The girl came quick, quick as thought, flung her arms round the old woman's neck and whispered, '*Oh grannie darling! It is such a lovely moon: do let me just go down to the boat with him and see poor Lennie*'. '*Run then, run, if you must have it so, you pretty wheedling tease; throw that shawl yonder over your head and be back in five minutes sharp like a good lass*'.

That *Graciosa* returned within the time specified, I will by no means take it upon me to aver; I leave it an open question to be decided by the expert reader at his or her own sweet will. But when she did return and bade the old lady a loving goodnight, there was something in her manner, and on her finger, that prompted her foster-mother to say once again, '*Ah Gracie, my pretty innocent, was there ever a young man that didn't care for sweets*'.

Glad at heart, a proud and happy man was Peter Gray that sweet autumnal night. The blushing girl had given her consent that fateful hour and he was now an accepted lover. The ring of betrothal had been slipped on the girl's finger, her lips had received the young man's shower of kisses, their troth had been plighted under shadow of the hoary water-gate and all in those delicious 'five minutes' of grace. Marriage loomed large ahead; and there was every prospect of Peter's being able, by Christmas, to deck his breezy home on the hill with the fairest flower of all the country-side.

Without doubt, as the two brothers pull homeward, the thoughts of the elder dwelt peacefully on the coming bliss; but ere they reached their destination, he was rudely wakened from his reverie by a sudden change of weather and his thoughts now centred on the management of their boat. They ran her ashore in a sandy cove, south of their house and sending Lennie forward to announce their return to the anxious mother Peter himself remained behind to look to the unloading of their craft and bring the packages home at leisure. '*Keep a bit of supper for me lad,*' he called after his brother's retiring figure, '*and get thee to thy bed. Give my love to my mother: if she cares to bide by the fire awhile, I have news to cheer her heart*'.

'*But bless me Lennie what ails thy brother that he lags so far behind?*' cried the widow when their supper was done and the clock struck twelve.

Lennie, with a frightened glance at the clock, sprang up and hurried outside. His loud halloas broke the silence of the night, but there was none to answer from below. At break-neck speed he slid down a zigzag in the cliff-side to where their boat lay high and dry, but no Peter was there. Time drew on to that darkest hour before the dawn, the moon was set already, her light extinct in total darkness, and still no news of Peter.

The distracted mother, lantern in hand, joined her son on the beach and cast about in vain to find the missing man. By the dim wick of rushlight they tracked his footprints along the level sand to the entry of a huge, open cave, whose yawning mouth is fed by every flow of tide. Here they lost all trace of Peter and his fate: he was never more seen alive.

In all probability he had stumbled unawares on the fierce bandits of the cave, hard at their illicit task, been taken in the gloom for a coastguard and done away with accordingly. The smugglers, it is true, strenuously denied all knowledge of the missing lad in a subsequent interview with Lennie, but Lennie harkened not to their glozing tongues; while, as for the distracted mother, she in her agony and wild despair called down God's curse on the whole crew and to her dying day cried aloud for vengeance. Her cry was heard in Heaven, her prayer was answered, her revenge was ample; but it came, alas, too late, for with her first born's loss the widow lost all heart, pined fast away, and sank ere long into a wished for grave. She bequeathed her Lennie this dying legacy *'Remember poor Peter'* and with those words on her lips, passed to her account.

The news of Peter's disappearance spread like wildfire. A sharp hue and cry was raised; men with bloodhounds scoured the country-side; others with grapnels went afloat and raked the ocean-bed to hook the sunken body. Their quest was in vain and a day came when they ceased to search. But it was not possible that our sweet *Graciosa* could be kept long in ignorance of what was the whole town's talk. In vain day after day did she look for the coming of her lover; in vain did she listen for his well known step or knock.

At length old Phoebe, gently as might be, broke the fatal news to her. The poor child received it humbly, without a tear. There was an alarming calmness and self-possession in her manner that boded ill. All she said was *'I shall see him again, I shall see him again'*. Her friends attributed this great meekness and gentleness of spirit to pious resignation and submission to the Divine will, for she had been, as had they all, in the July of that year, to hear Mr John Wesley preach in the High Street of their native town and his words and manner had made a deep impression on her heart. Old Phoebe, I think, knew better from the first. The simple truth was that *Graciosa's* heart was broken. From the day of that fateful news she seemed to pine away in mind and body both. She said very little to anyone now, but would murmur, sometimes with a sigh, sometimes with a smile, *'I shall see him again, I shall see him again'*.

Her workaday clothes were laid aside; very likely, poor girl, she knew that work, for her, was over in this world. She ever dressed herself in the things that her Peter had loved best to see her in, and, thus attired, she would spend hours of the day and of the night sauntering on the wall or the pier, gazing seawards and softly saying to herself '*I shall see him again*'. Remembering the glorious beauty and comeliness they had so lately worshipped, her present condition begot in the rough men of the place a sort of superstitious reverence and awe. '*Ah poor innocent*' they would say as she flitted past them in the gloaming, '*that it should have come to this. God help us all and send the girl her wits*'. Stalwart pilots would lead her home tenderly and she would go meekly when led; but she had lost all reckoning of hours and knowledge of time.

All that autumn she continued fading away and when the swallows were fled and the last leaves gone it was well seen that she would not linger long behind.

The merry time of Yule drew on apace. On the Sunday afternoon next before the feast, people were lounging over the sea-wall, disporting themselves in the frosty sunshine or watching the strong indraught of flood-tide that raced round the Heugh, and, passing in a strong deep current at their feet, flowed up into the estuary beyond. Suddenly, in their midst stood *Graciosa*, the pallor of death in her cheeks, her great lustrous eyes shining with clairvoyant brilliance, and having in their expression that dreamy, far away look of second-sight. Little heeding the idlers she moved among, the girl paced slowly on along the wall above the water-gate, gazing steadily seawards, still murmuring to herself, '*I shall see him again*'.

Many followed her gaze, under some occult sympathy or mesmerist fascination; and it appeared at last there really was something to gaze at. Their attention was riveted, their eyes fixed, on a something, they knew not what. '*A seal*' said one; '*A spar on end*' said another; '*A buoy broke loose and coming in with the tide*' suggested a third. They had not long to wait in suspense; the tide ran fast and full and the object of their conjectures moved quickly up till it came abreast of the place where they stood; then meeting with some entanglement below, it made a halt, and, turning itself round to the company on the water-gate with *Graciosa* in their midst, it bobbed and bowed and grinned and curtseyed, turning its sightless sockets on the very spot where *Graciosa* stood. The hair was all fallen off but it had clothed its scalp with a tangle of sea-wrack and diaphanous weed that glinted and glittered like an iris in the setting sun. While all stood speechless and horror struck, it freed itself from the entanglement below, and, making a final bow to the company as it tugged itself clear, swept silently on with the tide to the estuary above the town. In the awful hush and silence of the crowd, *Graciosa* was heard saying faintly '*I have seen him again*'.

Good women, sobbing, led the tearless girl away. She was faint and weak now and glad to be helped to bed. When the women were gone their ways and old Phoebe and she had the chamber to themselves, she said very calmly '*I shall wear that dress no more; but keep it from the fretting moth, for Peter's sake and mine. When next I leave this closet bed, in which I was born, I shall wear a different dress*'.

Her granny, hoping against hope and half minded to think this is the glimmer of returning reason and interest in life, inquired what dress she would choose to wear. *'A shroud'*. She replied to the poor woman's dismay; nor was she pacified till she had seen the flannel brought out from its chest and made up into that grim, horrid garb of burial. Then she seemed easier in her mind and said she was ready to go. After that she wandered in her talk. Sometimes she would say, with a shudder, as the weeping women stood round her dying bed waiting for the end, *'I have seen him again'*. At other and happier moments with a smile *'I shall see him again'*. With these last words of hope on her lips she passed quietly away to join her lover as the clock on the steeple chimed eight on Christmas Day morning. It was a sad Christmas they kept that day in the old port of Hartlepool, a day of dolour and complaint with cries of woe and loud lamentation.

Late on Christmas Eve searchers had come across that risen body, stranded in the slime and ooze of the estuary, shreds of shirt still clinging to its back and a weight of rolled lead (such as tea is wrapped in) tied to its heels: and now on this Christmas Day, while men were following the remains of Peter Gray to their last resting place in the churchyard of St Hilda, pious women were laying out the dead girl's body and arraying her for the short journey that lay between her and her lover's grave. They dressed her, not in that ugly shroud, but in those clothes Peter had loved so well; and very lovely her wax-like figure looked lying in the open coffin with many candles burning in the darkened chamber. On her finger she still wore the ring of engagement and in her hand she clasped a little crucifix of her dead mother's. On the breast of the corpse they placed a pewter dish of salt. This is one of the quaint local customs that still maintain their ground, despite the attacks of a so-called enlightenment. Its origin is lost in the mists of antiquity.

For two nights, strict watch was kept round the yawning grave in the churchyard, men relieving one another by turns, with a flare-up of resinous chips in an open iron cage. On the third day, at sunset, the great bell tolled with heavy boom across the bay and the street was thronged to see *Graciosa* borne to her lover's side. Girls in white strewed bay-leaves before her and they sang psalms as they moved slowly up the hilly street. At the gate they were met by Mr Crookbain, who read the Prayers for the Dead so simply and so feelingly that there was not one dry eye left among that vast concourse of mourners.

A tombstone was set up, at the public cost, to mark the spot of consecrated earth where the bodies lay; and those who choose may yet go to the wind-swept churchyard on the cliff and see for themselves the simple epitaph that records the faithful loves and piteous fates of Peter Gray and *Graciosa*.

Sources

Description of those Highly Notable Watering Places in the County of Durham, Hartlepool and Seaton Carew, including a short account of the village of Stranton. William Tate, 1812

The History and Antiquities of the County Palatine of Durham. William Hutchinson, 1785

The History and Antiquities of the County Palatine of Durham. Robert Surtees. Vol III, 1823

Local Records of Stockton & Neighbourhood. T Richmond, 1868

History, Topography and Directory of Durham. Whellan, London, 1894

Fell's Guide to Sunken Treasure, 1969

West Hartlepool. Robert Wood, 1967

Cliff House Pottery, West Hartlepool. Phillip J Duce, 1992

A Hartlepool Chronology. John M Ward, 1999

An Architectural History. Hartlepool Civic Society, 2000

Whellan's Directory of Durham, 1885–1900

The Hutchinson Concise Encyclopedia, 1999

Durham Chronicle, 1815

South Durham Herald

Stockton & Cleveland Mercury

Northern Garland

Northern Daily Mail

Hartlepool Mail

Acknowledgements

Gemma Callahan, Anne Allen and Syd Neville of Bowes Museum. Deborah Anderson and Ann Biggs of Bowes Museum Archaeology Department. John W Perrin. John H Proud. George Colley. Arthur Brougham, Hartlepool Yacht Club. Gary Green of Tees Archaeology. Charlotte Taylor of Hartlepool Arts & Museum Collection. Hartlepool Reference Library staff. John C Harrison.

Index